The
TARANTULA
Keeper's Guide

The
TARANTULA
Keeper's Guide

Stanley A. Schultz

Sterling Publishing Co. Inc. New York
Distributed in the U.K. by Blandford Press

Library of Congress Cataloging in Publication Data

Schultz, Stanley A.
  The tarantula keeper's guide.

  Bibliography: p.
  Includes index.
  1. Tarantulas as pets. 2. Tarantulas. I. Title
SF459.T37S38   1984   639.7   83-24289
ISBN 0-8069-3122-1
ISBN 0-8069-7854-6 (pbk.)

Copyright © 1984 by Sterling Publishing Co., Inc.
Two Park Avenue, New York, N.Y. 10016
Distributed in Australia by Oak Tree Press Co., Ltd.
P.O. Box K514 Haymarket, Sydney 2000, N.S.W.
Distributed in the United Kingdom by Blandford Press
Link House, West Street, Poole, Dorset BH15 1LL, England
Distributed in Canada by Oak Tree Press Ltd.
% Canadian Manda Group, P.O. Box 920, Station U
Toronto, Ontario, Canada M8Z 5P9
Manufactured in the United States of America

Contents

Preface

There is a need to know.

Literally thousands of tarantulas are captured and sold in the pet industry every year (Browning, 1981), and the number increases year by year. Many of these die of neglect or, even worse, of misguided care when they easily could have made harmless, interesting pets. Many more are destroyed in nature because of man's ignorance or superstition.

This should not be.

This book is intended to satisfy that need to know. To date there have been almost no authoritative works available to the general public on these fascinating animals. Whether you were a junior high school student seeking material for a term paper, an arachnophobe seeking to allay your neurosis, or a hobbyist trying to learn more about your pets, you had almost no place to garner the information you required outside of scattered, mostly unavailable scientific papers buried in the dark recesses of only the largest libraries. You might spend days, weeks, even months searching for the references you needed, only to find that they did not contain the information you wanted. I know, I've done it!

When I decided to write a popular book about tarantulas an entire library of information was expected—something at least comparable to what has been written about snakes, for instance.

However, all such expectations were quickly dashed. The total scientific literature dealing with tarantulas is more comparable to a medium-sized telephone directory. Thus my task turned from distilling volumes of facts to ferreting out every one available.

This paucity of scientific knowledge is due, I am sure, to the fact that there is little economic importance to tarantulas. By far their most lucrative aspects, in North America at least, have been their sales in the pet industry (Browning, 1981) and their stardom in the movies. But neither characteristic is the type that begets large research grants.

While every man, woman, and child in the modern world knows *of* tarantulas, few really know anything *about* tarantulas. What little is known about them somehow doesn't sift down very readily from the lofty, often stuffy, scientific literature, and most of us remain abysmally ignorant or, even worse, steeped in old wives' tales.

Thus I have three purposes for writing this book. First, to relay information, as there is a real need for an in-depth treatment of what a tarantula really is and how one should be cared for. Second, to stimulate the reader to find out more about these animals in the hope that his enthusiasm will infect others. Third, to show the hobbyist where the limits of our knowledge are and where he may expand them.

This book is not intended to be a shallow, trivial treatment of the subject. In fact, in many places the text will become quite technical. This cannot be helped as the subject matter will be totally new and foreign to most readers. Take heart. If you don't understand a passage don't let it bog you down. Finish reading the book, then go back and reread the troublesome parts. If they are still not clear to you, you may consult some of the references or discuss the terms with someone who knows them (a biology teacher, for instance). It is not intended that you should be able to absorb all the information in this book on the first reading, or even the second. But rather, it is intended that this information be readily available to you in a concise form when you need it.

Throughout the text, usually enclosed in parentheses, occur

names with dates. These refer to specific entries in the bibliography. A major shortcoming of most tarantula books is the absence of such a reference list. I hope this addition will help the interested hobbyist, student, or arachnophobe locate further reading material. Most of these references will not be locally available to you, but your library probably will be able to acquire copies for you through an interlibrary loan system. As you read through these books and papers you will find many more references that were not mentioned in this book. Also, be sure to check the newer issues of those periodicals mentioned. There is some continuing research being done on tarantulas.

Everyone who has ever purchased a pet tarantula has helped in the writing of this book, and to them I offer my deepest gratitude. A few people do deserve special mention, however. Among them are Paul Christ for proofreading the manuscript, John and Brenda Blue for the detailed information about their "blessed event," David Mallow for his help in identifying the mites, and Ron Wilson for the report of his "skinny dipping" tarantula. Mildred Lynch and Cleopatra were especially important in the section on health problems. Paul Manger acted as the catalyst for this book. And, David Mask should receive special mention for allowing me to photograph the Costa Rican tarantulas as well as for proofreading the manuscript.

The tarantula design on Delbert Richburg's T-shirt was by Karl Dallas Wegener, and the line drawings were done by Deidre L. Tomkins. All photos are by the author unless credited otherwise.

I would also like to express my appreciation to the Upjohn Company of Kalamazoo, Michigan, for the kind permission to use its registered trademarks in this book.

I must surely have left out some other most important people. To them I can only offer my sincerest apologies and thanks.

Lastly, and most especially, I would like to offer much thanks and appreciation to my wife, Marguerite, for the hard work that she gladly gave through all the years of tarantula keeping, and for her help in the preparation of this book. She would have been listed as coauthor had she not so firmly declined. If it were not for her words of encouragement, and occasional prodding, you would not be reading this book today.

Stanley A. Schultz
Galveston, Texas

1
The Tarantula Myth

There is something mysterious about tarantulas. They startle people. They're creatures of the night, magically appearing and then disappearing into the dark again. They have long, hairy legs and appear huge and forbidding. But foremost, they're spiders!

Because of all this it is natural that superstitious man should credit them with all sorts of sinister properties. And where fact does not exist myth runs rampant. As a result tarantula lore is a very fertile field.

The very name "tarantula" is a misnomer. There is a spider, belonging to an unrelated group, which became famous during the fifteenth century. This spider is named after the Italian town of Taranto (Tarantum to Renaissance man) and is credited with causing a strange condition called "Tarantism" (Gertsch, 1979). By legend, the bite of this spider was blamed for the disease, and anyone suffering the malady was obliged, as the only cure, to engage in a frenzied, feverish dance—virtually a Renaissance discotheque!

As a result, any large spider was suspect and much feared by the peasantry. As Renaissance man explored the world he would return with fearsome tales of giant spiders, "tarantulas," all through the tropics, subtropics, and warmer temperate zones. Gradually, English-speaking people, especially Americans, applied the name to a group of much larger and more spectacular spiders than the one from Europe, forgetting almost entirely about Taranto and Tarantism. The myth of large, dangerous spiders still persists even today. Interestingly, most Europeans refer to our tarantulas as "Mygales" or "Vogelspinnen." This latter name means "bird spider" in German and refers to the fact that a few tropical, arboreal species have been observed to catch and eat small birds, although to what extent still isn't known.

To make matters even more complicated, there is another animal, only very distantly related to spiders, which carries the scientific name of *Tarantula,* but is neither a spider nor venomous. For now we will simply state that what we mean by the term "tarantula" is a collection of several different kinds of extremely large, hairy spiders that usually live in burrows; and leave a more precise definition for a later chapter.

Most generally, the layman confuses tarantulas with black widow spiders (see Color Illus. Q), thus enhancing the myth. Even worse, there are a few species of tarantulas and some of their close allies that are dangerous (Bucherl, 1968; Maratic, 1967), thus adding fuel to the fire.

Tarantulas have gotten a lot of "bad press" in the movies, too. At least six movies, starring such noted actors as Sean Connery, The Three Stooges, and William Shatner, have featured tarantulas as menaces to civilization or humanity. "The Tarantula That Ate Tokyo" is a long-standing joke among horror-movie aficionados. The fact is these movies play with the ignorance and fears passed on for generations by unenlightened people. Nobody would pay to see the movie "The Beagle Who Ate Boston" since everybody knows what a beagle really is. Few know tarantulas as well.

Almost every property attributed to tarantulas by these movies is in direct contradiction to reality. While such movies may be recommended as entertainment they must also be recommended as detailed accounts of what tarantulas are not.

The following list of tall stories about tarantulas is offered for the reader's entertainment and enlightenment.

"I almost died from that tarantula's bite!" Tarantulas seldom bite. In general, if a tarantula isn't openly hostile or panic-stricken you may assume that it will not bite when touched. Even if a tarantula does bite it seldom injects any venom. And, even if venom is injected, the effect is hardly worth mentioning except for its rarity. As near as can be determined, all serious spider bites recorded in the United States are from either black widow spiders or brown recluse spiders. Out of ignorance and with the help of horror movies, the layman persistently confuses these two dangerous species with tarantulas even though there is little or no resemblance.

"That tarantula jumped twenty-five feet!" As will be explained more fully later in this book, tarantulas are physically incapable of launching themselves more than a very few inches. Even if long-distance jumps were possible their body walls would not be able to absorb the force of impact as they landed. They would "splat" like rotten tomatoes! One impetuous leap would end it all. This is clearly not a survival characteristic.

"I swear that tarantula was three feet across!" The largest tarantula of record only spanned ten inches (Gertsch, 1979), and was a male and therefore had much longer legs and a lighter body than its corresponding female. Even then, it was truly formidable to be sure! But because of the limitations of their construction it is doubtful that any will be found that are much larger. In the excitement of the moment an objective size appraisal cannot be expected from the casual observer who is startled by a large spider. This is especially true if he has a deep-seated, superstitious fear of them. Spider stories, like fish stories, tend to grow with age—and with the gullibility of the audience.

"The tarantula bit him while he sat on the latrine!" While tarantulas are capable of limited climbing they certainly aren't comfortable at it. They are just too heavy to attempt vertical surfaces, much less hang from the underside of a latrine seat. Furthermore, latrines and privies are very nearly the most unlikely places imaginable for one to find a tarantula, for their lifestyles are such that there is nothing in such a habitat to attract them. The question of their biting has already been discussed. Typical latrine bites, and those in other outbuildings, are far more characteristic of black widow or brown recluse spiders. Not only are these far more common in such situations, but the bites' symptoms match far better (Parrish, 1959).

Furthermore, once and for all:
    Tarantulas do not ravish fair maidens!
    Tarantulas do not cause Tarantism!
    Tarantulas do not embalm people or towns!
      and lastly,
    Tarantulas did not eat Tokyo!

Tarantulas, then, are the fall guys. Misnamed, falsely accused, slandered, and convicted without a trial, these gentle giants of the spider world still persist, oblivious to it all, waiting at the mouths of their lairs for another beetle.

Fortunately, man is learning. There is still hope.

2

The Physical Tarantula

ANATOMY

Tarantulas belong to a vast group of very successful animals called arthropods. As with most other arthropods they possess a thick hide or shell called an exoskeleton. This exoskeleton has a rather complex layered construction with many folds and indentations. It is composed of many different substances. Among them is chitin, which is responsible for the exoskeleton's tough, leathery properties. Chemically, chitin is a nitrogenous polysaccharide (complex sugar) somewhat similar to cellulose in plants. Another important substance is a scleroprotein. Hard portions are said to be sclerotized, that is, laden with heavy concentrations of calcium compounds (Meglitch, 1972). This exoskeleton appears to be a suit of armor superficially resembling a medieval knight's, with each plate having a unique shape, position, function, and name. It is the most fundamental characteristic of the entire group of arthropods, and it influences virtually every aspect of their lives.

Structure. Tarantulas have no "head," "thorax," or "abdomen" in the same sense as humans. Their bodies are divided into two obvious body parts: the forward prosoma and the rearward

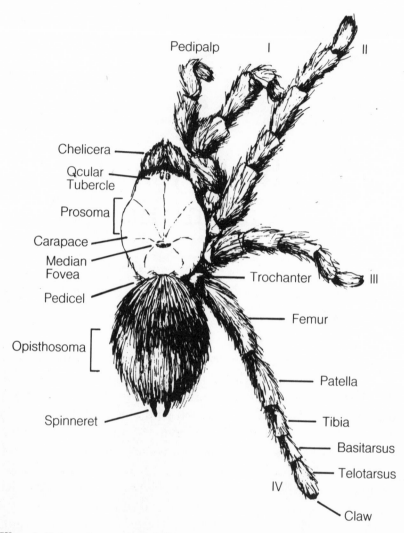

Illus. 1. External anatomy of a tarantula, dorsal view. (See page 27 for a ventral view.)

opisthosoma (Illus. 1). These are connected by a narrow "hourglass" constriction called the pedicel (peduncle in some books).

While the prosoma has been likened to a fused head and thorax (cephalothorax), the opisthosoma to an abdomen, and the pedicel to a waist, these comparisons are not accurate and carry misleading connotations. The organization of the animal's internal organs does not follow the conventions assumed by these labels, therefore we use the terms prosoma, opisthosoma, and pedicel instead. A little practice at pronouncing them will make even the novice sound like a "pro."

The back plate of the prosoma is the heavily sclerotized carapace, with the smaller "chest" shield being called the sternum. Both are bounded by the basal segments of the legs, called coxae (singular: coxa). There are little oval bare spots called sigilla (singular: sigillum) on the sternum near the bases of the coxae. Their purpose, if any, seems to be a total mystery.

The opisthosoma is usually globose (bulging, round) and is covered with a thin, leathery exoskeleton with no obvious plates or seams. It is clothed with a dense layer of bristles which will be discussed shortly.

Appendages. Tarantulas have a grand total of eight pairs of appendages on their bodies. The very first pair on the front end are a pair of chelicerae (singular: chelicera) (Illus. 2 and 3). While these

Illus. 2. Face to face with a tarantula. Compare the ocular tubercle and the attachment of the chelicerae with the wolf spider in Illus. 17 (page 46).

Illus. 3. Chelicera and fang. In the fringe of bristles are strong teeth against which the fang closes.

are probably homologous with the jaws of insects and crustaceans, they now serve a somewhat different purpose. Eons ago, on spiders' precursors, these were probably leglike appendages used for guidance when moving, as well as for subduing and manipulating food. However, as spiders evolved, these become reduced and modified to resemble a single heavy finger joint with a clawlike fang hinged to the end, somewhat reminiscent of a cat's toe and claw. These fangs are very heavily sclerotized hypodermic needles with a passageway leading back up into the chelicerae to the venom glands. In present day spiders they are weapons, pure and simple.

Tarantulas do not have antennae. Instead, as the chelicerae evolved into weapons, the next pair of appendages took over their tactile duties and became the pedipalps (Illus. 4). While they resemble legs they have only one claw at the tip rather than two, and they appear to have one less segment. As we shall see shortly, the latter is not necessarily true.

Illus. 4. Pedipalp and legs, in order, from one side of a male tarantula, pedipalp towards the top. The tip of the female's pedipalp resembles that of a leg.

The pedipalps act as "feelers," probing and guiding as the animal moves or eats. In male spiders they are something else—they are sex organs. More about this will be said later. The bases of these pedipalps may be toothed or ridged to aid in masticating (chewing) food. The bristles and hairs on them may be used for straining food. Their segments are named, from body outwards: coxa, trochanter, femur, patella, tibia, tarsus, and pretarsus or claw.

The next four pairs of appendages are the walking legs. Tarantulas have eight legs just like all other spiders. Each of these is composed of six tubular segments separated by pliable leathery "hinges," plus a seventh which is little more than an end plate bearing two pads of bristles and two claws (Illus. 5). There appear to be eight segments (or articles). However, one segment, the tarsus, is superficially divided into two pseudosegments which are not moved by muscles. Therefore, there are actually only seven hinges, and seven segments. Starting from the prosoma they are: coxa, trochanter, femur, patella, tibia, tarsus (basitarsus + telotarsus), and pretarsus or claws (Snodgrass, 1967). Thus, it would

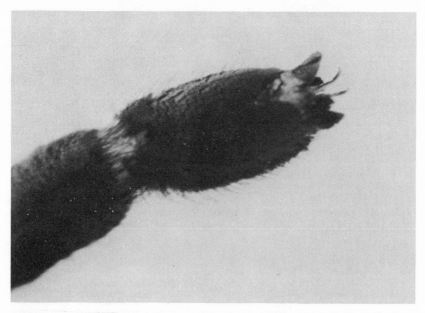

Illus. 5. Pretarsus and claws of a tarantula's leg. Note, too, the pads of bristles on each side.

appear that the legs have one more segment than the pedipalps; but in truth pedipalps and legs have the same number!

There is some disagreement about the naming of these segments, with some authors using alternate names. The reader is cautioned against being confused by this.

Some tarantulas (particularly some Old World species) have sclerotized rods and teeth on the trochanters of their pedipalps and the outer surfaces of their chelicerae. They scrape these together to produce a loud rasping or buzzing sound when they feel threatened. This sound is called stridulation and is the loudest sound that tarantulas can make. Some hobbyists report a "swishing," "brushing," or "thumping" sound when their pet tarantulas are startled. This has not yet been reported in the scientific literature but may be a ploy used to startle predators. Here is a chance for the hobbyist to contribute to man's knowledge. By careful observation and perhaps a strategically placed tape recorder we may be able to catalogue these sounds and determine how they are produced. Is there really more than one type of sound? Do the sounds' characteristics differ with sex? Species? Age? Some other factor? Can tarantulas hear? Do they use these sounds during courtship? In signalling other tarantulas of danger?

All of the appendages mentioned so far have been attached to the tarantula's prosoma. The last two pairs are the only ones attached to the animal's opisthosoma. These are the spinnerets on the rear. One pair is very short and hardly discernible. However, the other pair is much larger and resembles a pair of very delicate fingers. All four produce silk from silk glands inside the opisthosoma.

Bristles. While tarantulas appear to be covered with hairs, we must remember that these are actually dead, nongrowing bristles rather than continually growing hair in the mammalian sense.

The bristles on the top rear of many species are loosely attached and bedecked with varying patterns of backward-pointing barbs. Currently, four distinct types are recognized. In all but one type, the unattached end is sharply pointed and works as a small harpoon. These bristles break off with very little effort and the tarantula, with its hind legs, uses this facility to brush them into the

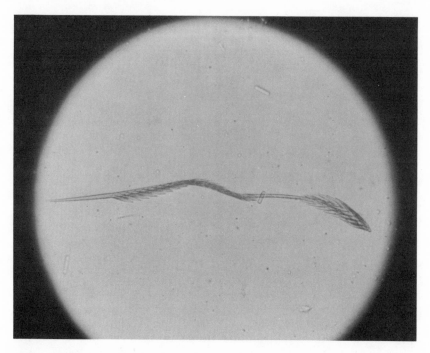

Illus. 6. One type of urticating bristle, attached to the tarantula by the left end. The sharp right end is the penetrating end. About 0.23 mm long.

face of predators. As the bristles penetrate they cause much irritation and are thus termed urticating bristles or hairs. Also, in at least one type there is a short segment towards the rear containing *forward*-pointing barbs which insure that the bristles will only penetrate far enough to do the greatest harm, and then remain there (Illus. 6).

Studies have shown that the irritating properties of these bristles are due at least in part to an irritating chemical on or in them. No one has yet determined the exact composition of this substance, however. Some of the itching powder once sold in novelty shops was, in reality, tarantula hair. A coyote or mouse that is harassing a tarantula is courting a severe bout of red, itching eyes and violent sneezing. Meanwhile, the tarantula makes good its escape.

Recently, the structure of these hairs has been given much importance as a taxonomic tool (Cook, et al, 1972). Curiously, most

New World tarantulas possess urticating bristles, lack stridulating organs, and are relatively docile. By contrast, most Old World species lack urticating hairs, possess stridulating organs, and can be quite pugnacious. This is presumed to evidence two different tacks that were taken to deal with the problem of predation and self-preservation. To date no one has made an attempt to closely correlate geographic origin with these structure and habit-pattern differences; and they cannot be used as hard and fast rules for determining the origin of any given tarantula.

Internal Structure. Internally, tarantulas have no skeleton, but possess an exoskeleton which is folded and ridged to provide strength and to allow for the attachment of muscles. It should be noted here that the basic principle behind this exoskeleton has been around for more than a half-billion years, a lot longer than our internal or endoskeleton. By far the most successful group of animals on earth, the arthropods use the exoskeleton. You can't argue with simplicity *and* success!

Nervous System. The tarantula's nervous system is composed of a radiating array of nerve fibres originating from a brain which lies on the floor of the prosoma—in their "chests" so to speak. It is quite large, nearly as long and as wide as the sternum shield. From this brain, heavy nerve cords connect to the organs and appendages in the prosoma, and one major nerve cord passes through the pedicel into the opisthosoma. Thus the brain is a concentrated, centralized seat of authority in tarantulas, as opposed to the rather diffuse system of nerve cords and ganglia in most arthropods.

On the top of the prosoma, towards the front, is a small elevation resembling a cupola or turret. This is called the ocular tubercle and it holds the eight simple eyes or ocelli (singular: ocellus) (Illus. 7). These are connected to the brain by optic nerves.

If tarantulas are capable of forming an image with their eyes it is of dubious value. They spend most of their lives in dark burrows, coming out only at dusk. Even then, their eyes are situated inside a circle of legs—they see mostly "knees." However, wild tarantulas, or those not accustomed to handling, do react to motions around them. They will turn to face an approaching hand

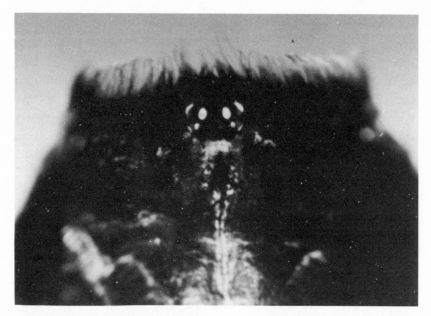

Illus. 7. The eye field of a tarantula from inside the carapace.

or take flight from an approaching animal. Thus their eyes are functional and the tarantulas do make use of them.

Many of the bristles on a tarantula's body, setae, and trichobothria (singular: seta and trichobothrium) are connected to nerve endings which lead to the brain and are very sensitive tactile organs. In addition, there are many enigmatic, microscopic structures situated among these bristles that may be chemoreceptors or thermo-receptors. While some serious research has been done on some of these sensory structures (Den Otter, 1974) there is still much that we do not know.

Can tarantulas distinguish colors? Can they distinguish shapes? Do they taste? Smell? Do they feel pain? Do they have senses that we aren't aware of? What role do any of these play in their day-to-day lives? The magnitude of our ignorance is staggering.

Circulation. A tarantula's circulatory system is open. This means that their arteries and veins are not interconnected by capillaries to become a closed system, and their blood moves more or less freely through their tissues. The blood and body fluids of the tarantula are one and the same and is called hemolymph. It is "slurped" up through four pairs of pores, called ostia, along the length of the long, tubular heart, which lies along the top center of the opisthosoma (Illus. 8). The hemolymph from the heart is then piped forward by means of an artery through the pedicel into the prosoma. There it is distributed by arterial branches and released into cavities and spaces in the tissues and organs. It oozes through the tissues and is collected by veins which pass back through the pedicel into the opisthosoma to the book lungs, described below. The hemolymph is again collected in the pericardium, the tubular chamber which holds the heart and acts as a staging area preparatory to having the hemolymph cycled through again.

Tarantulas are poikilothermic; that is, cold-blooded. Their heart rates, hemolymph flow, and pressures are at least partially dependent on their activity levels and temperatures. Not enough research has been done to determine precisely how these are in-

Illus. 8. Dissection of a tarantula. In the prosoma (left) are large muscle masses surrounding the pumping stomach. In the opisthosoma (right) are pale food storage tissue and the dark median heart and pericardium. The larger two of the four spinnerets are obvious at the end of the opisthosoma.

terrelated. As will be seen later, hemolymph pressures are even more important to spiders than they are to most other animals.

The oxygen-carrying pigment in hemolymph is hemocyanin and uses copper in its binding site (Ghiretti-Magaldi and Tamino, 1977; Linzen, et al, 1977; Loewe, et al, 1977). This is in contrast to hemoglobin with iron in man. Neither is the hemocyanin contained in blood corpuscles as in man. It is dissolved directly in the hemolymph. There are perhaps four types of ameboid white corpuscles which wander through the animal's tissues, but their function is poorly understood. They appear somewhat similar to various white corpuscles in our own blood and we presume that they engulf invading organisms before they can cause disease. One important function that mammalian leucocytes have is the production of antibodies. At this time little or no information is available to indicate whether or not a spider's white blood cells are capable of a similar function.

Well-oxygenated hemolymph has a distinct bluish cast, not red as in hemoglobin. Ordinarily a tarantula's hemolymph is nearly colorless and odorless, but feels slippery and slightly sticky, very much like our blood. Of particular interest, the hemolymph of spiders and scorpions is quite toxic when injected into small mammals (Savory, 1964).

Respiration. Tarantulas breathe by means of four book lungs (Illus. 9 and 10). These resemble pockets on the bottom of their opisthosomas similar to the back pockets on your blue jeans. The slitlike openings are called spiracles. If you pick up a tarantula and turn it over you should be able to see at least the rear pair. Sometimes the forward pair is indistinct. Internally, they contain sheetlike folds of thin membrane which resemble the pages of a partially open book. Hemolymph circulates inside these sheets, exchanging carbon dioxide for oxygen with the air that separates them.

Most arachnologists believe that spiders do not inhale or exhale, but rather that air merely diffuses passively in and out of the book lungs (Snodgrass, 1952). However, during autopsy, this author has noted large muscle masses attached to the book lungs or in their immediate proximity. Could they be used for ventilating

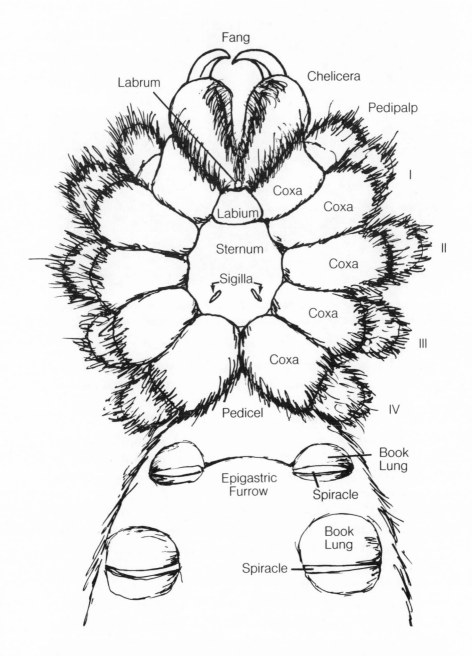

Illus. 9. External anatomy of a tarantula, ventral view. (See page 16 for a dorsal view.)

Illus. 10. Interior of the opisthosoma of a cast skin. Four white book lungs are easily seen. The epigastric furrow connects the forward pair (right).

the book lungs? Could the tarantula's large size and consequent higher respiratory demands have obliged it to develop a method for increasing airflow past these organs? Or could the persistent weight of a bulbous opisthosoma on the highly compressible book lungs necessitate a muscular apparatus for keeping them open? Contrary to popular scientific opinion, do tarantulas actually breathe? Only further work by competent researchers can answer these questions.

Digestion. Tarantulas have no jaws. They rely on their heavily sclerotized chelicerae, their fangs, and the bases of their pedipalps to crush their prey. They seldom use their venom unless their prey is too large or aggressive. Their throats are so small that they cannot swallow pieces of food. Instead, they regurgitate digestive fluids while masticating (chewing) their prey. The resulting liquid mixture is drawn up through the mouth and pharynx (throat) by means of a powerful pumping stomach (Illus. 11).

The mouth lies between the bases of the pedipalps' coxae and immediately above a small plate called the labium, or lower lip.

The labium appears to be a small forward extension of the sternum. Above the mouth, between the bases of the chelicerae, is the labrum, or upper lip.

The principal muscles for the operation of the pumping stomach are attached to the center of the carapace, which is deeply infolded to allow a firm place of attachment for them. This area appears as a dent, called the median fovea, in the middle of the carapace. The carapace is also thickened and arched to sustain the force.

The pumping stomach passes the juices downwards into a true stomach where they are further digested and at least partially absorbed. This true stomach lies between the pumping stomach and the brain in the prosoma. Fingerlike projections, gastric ceca (singular: cecum), extend from the true stomach out into the bases of the legs.

The true stomach empties into a straight intestine which passes through the pedicel into the opisthosoma. Further digestion takes

Illus. 11. Dissection of the prosoma. The needle points out the pumping stomach. Beneath it lies the pale true stomach, under which is hidden the brain.

place there. Waste products are added towards the rear from the organs called Malpighian tubules. The excrement is then periodically voided through an anus which is located immediately above the spinnerets.

The principal waste product is guanine, a condition which is unique with spiders (Anderson, 1964; Rao and Gopalakrishnareddy, 1962). This is in direct contrast with most other animals which excrete some combination of ammonia, urea, uric acid, and allantoin.

Most arthropods possess coxal glands which are direct homologues (having similar origins and developments) of more primitive excretory organs called nephridia, and are found in less-advanced invertebrates. Tarantulas are no exception. They have two pairs located in the prosoma and emptying through pores in the animals' first and third coxae, whence the name. However, whether they are truly functional, what they excrete, and how important they are to the animal is still unclear. Regardless, it is still probably safe to say that tarantulas have no kidneys and do not urinate, at least in the normal sense.

Sex Organs. The sex life of tarantulas will be discussed later on. For now we mention that their gonads—ovaries in the female and testes in the male—are located inside the opisthosoma. Their genital openings are located under the opisthosoma along a groove, called the epigastric furrow, which runs crosswise between the forward pair of book lungs. As stated earlier, the male's intromittent organs are his pedipalps; he has no penis or anything homologous to one.

Motion. Tarantulas have a multitude of muscles. The prosoma is almost two-thirds filled with them and each leg has more than thirty. Yet they are nearly all retractors, designed only to pull the appendage towards the body. Then what extends the appendages? Hydraulic pressure! The pressure of the hemolymph is used to "inflate" the partially collapsed hinges at the joints of the legs in order to extend them (Ellis, 1944; Manton, 1958; Parry and Brown, 1959). The animal's heart apparently is capable of producing a hemolymph pressure comparable to human blood pressure and more. One report states a pressure of up to 260 mm of mercury (one-third atmospheric pressure!) in some species of spiders.

All this presents a serious design limitation. While the joints must be strong enough to withstand this pressure they must also remain pliable enough to allow free movement. For an animal as massive as a tarantula (by terrestrial arthropod standards) this tradeoff is crucial. The pressure required to lift their bodies more than a few inches would surely blow out all their joints. Further, if they became too large and massive they simply couldn't move. At the time of this writing the author has a huge female tarantula, of undetermined species, that weighs over 51 grams (1.8 ounces). She has become so large that she is incapable of righting herself when turned upside down on a smooth surface. Thus, all stories to the contrary not withstanding, tarantulas cannot launch themselves more than a very short distance, perhaps the length of their leg spans, without actually touching *terra firma*. And they probably would not be able to get much larger than the ten-inch Brazilian giant reported by Gertsch in 1979. They can, however, dart surprisingly fast for their mass.

While the tarantula's prosoma is filled primarily with muscle, stomachs, and brain, its opisthosoma is filled with gonads, heart, Malpighian tubules, silk glands, and fatty storage tissue, though not always in that order of abundance.

ECDYSIS (MOULTING)

The major disadvantage of a suit of armor is that it does not allow for its resident's growth. Eons ago, the tarantula's precursors solved this problem by periodically discarding the old, constraining shell. This poses a major problem because the only thing that contains and supports the animal is its exoskeleton. Without it the animal could not retain its physical integrity and would reduce to a blob of formless tissue.

A system had to be developed to allow the production of a new, larger, functional exoskeleton before the old one was discarded. The trick involves the production of a new shell just inside the

Illus. 12. The freshly cast skin of a tarantula. How much of the animal's anatomy can you identify?

old, shedding the old one (Illus. 12), inflating the new one while it is still reasonably pliable, then hardening it (see Color Illus. B, C, D, and E).

The entire process normally requires a year in adult tarantulas. For the sake of discussion, the process is divided into four phases: intermoult, premoult, moult, and postmoult. You must realize that it is a smooth, uninterrupted cycle with only very indistinct demarcations.

Illus. A. Pink-toed tarantula. This species is almost surely arboreal, and it is often sold as a bird-eating spider—which has yet to be demonstrated.

A

Illus. B. A tarantula in premoult. The bald area on the opistho-soma is very dark.

Illus. C. The beginning of moult. The tarantula has rolled over onto her back.

Illus. D. Moult. Still on her back, she is "ooz-ing" out of the old ex-oskeleton, which is held aloft here.

B

Illus. E. Postmoult and resting. The fangs and the hinge membranes on the legs are still pale but they will darken in a few hours.

Illus. F (left). Mexican cinnamon tarantula. Although infrequently imported, it makes an excellent pet. This one was presumed to be a female when the photo was taken. Illus. G (right). A male Mexican cinnamon tarantula. Believe it or not, this is the same animal shown in the photo at the left, but after a maturing molt. The change is very dramatic.

C

Illus. H. A pair of Mexican red-legged tarantulas, male on the left and female on the right. Contrast the male's pedipalps, femoral hooks, and general physique with that of the female.

Illus. J. Guatemalan black velvet tarantula.

Illus. I. Woolly Honduras tarantula.

D

Illus. K. This colorful Costa Rican tarantula should not be confused with the spiders in Illus. H—a lesson in why one cannot identify species by color pattern.

Illus. L. The Costa Rican gullwing tarantula, named for the peculiar stance it assumes when disturbed, is very excitable and is an extremely fast runner.

Illus. M. This is a dead tarantula. Contrast its pose to that of the moulting animal in Illus. C.

E

Illus. N. This "Rio Grande gold" tarantula, collected near Roma, Texas, made the bite shown below in Illus. O.

Illus. O. A tarantula bite. The author's right thumb with fang marks on the major knuckle. Very slight inflammation and almost no pain.

Illus. P. Dutchess, the mystery tarantula. What kind is she? Where is she native? Breeding programs are urgently needed for such species.

F

Illus. Q. The venomous black widow spider. Suborder Labidognatha, family Theridiidae. Lactrodectus mactans (*Fabricius*). *These dangerous spiders have given tarantulas an undeserved bad reputation.*

Illus. R (above). This Texas brown tarantula was collected in Texas, but the species is very common and widespread throughout the southwestern U.S. and northern Mexico. Illus. S (right). Haitian tarantula.

Illus. T. Becky Cole and the Dutchess. Mankind is not inherently fearful of spiders. That fear is an acquired trait.

Illus. U. Delbert Richburg and Cleopatra, his pet Mexican red leg. The T-shirt cartoon is an original design by Karl Dallas Wegener.

H

During most of the year a tarantula is in intermoult, the passive phase. However, usually during the summer or fall, the production of a sequence of specific hormones triggers the continuation of the moulting process. While these hormone control mechanisms are well known for insects and crustaceans (Burdette, 1974), little work has been done on spiders in general or tarantulas in particular.

Presumably the following is true. During premoult, a large portion of the sclerotizing calcium is withdrawn from the old exoskeleton and stored in the tarantula's internal organs. Then a new exoskeleton is grown just inside the old, between it and the ends of the muscles and nerves. Along with this new exoskeleton, an entirely new set of bristles is produced. Thus, if the animal were going "bald" (Illus. 13) because of the loss of a large portion of its urticating bristles, they would all be replaced at each moult. Clearly this is a survival characteristic.

Illus. 13. This Costa Rican tarantula shows an unusual pattern in which the urticating bristles were lost. The bare areas resemble two eye spots, possibly to confuse predators into believing that this is the head end.

After the new exoskeleton is nearly completed a liquid is secreted between it and the old exoskeleton, thus separating them. This entire phase requires more than a week, after which the tarantula may spin a bowl-shaped web, climb the edge of it, and roll backwards to lie upside down. Frequently, long-term captive tarantulas will not spin such a moulting cradle. Does this ever happen in nature? How do they moult in the confines of their burrows? We simply don't know, but the hobbyist, with carefully thought-out caging, might be able to discover and even photograph the answers to these questions.

During the next phase, called simply moult, with the animal upside down, the carapace loosens around its front and sides and is forced slowly out of the way. The tarantula, with its new, still pliable exoskeleton, miraculously eases out of the opening with a nearly imperceptible pumping action. The process may be roughly compared to a medieval knight backing out of his armor through the "trap." Moult may take nearly half a day, and after it is finished the tarantula may lie upside down several hours just resting. Eventually it will turn right side up. Take careful note: A tarantula that is lying on its back is probably moulting, *not* dying. Dying tarantulas almost never "keel over." They remain upright with their legs folded under them (see Color Illus. M).

In the next phase, postmoult, the new exoskeleton swells, possibly as a result of the animal swallowing air, and hardens. Thus the new shell, which was inside the old one and therefore smaller, expands to a size somewhat larger than the old one. For the next several days the exoskeleton hardens by the absorption of those calcium compounds that were stored in the internal organs. The lining of the mouth, pharynx, and pumping stomach are also shed, and the tarantula will not eat until these are also thoroughly sclerotized. This may require a week or more. The end of postmoult and the beginning of intermoult is signalled when the animal again accepts food.

These are among the most critical periods in the animal's life for the moulting process holds much risk.

In addition, during premoult the tarantula's sensory structures are presumably disconnected from the old exoskeleton. The effect might be the same as being totally covered by a thick plastic bag. Touch, smell, taste, and sight would all be drastically impaired and the tarantula could not sense predators effectively. At the same time, the old exoskeleton would tend to interfere with motion much the same as many layers of clothing would, slowing the animal's reaction time and reducing its ability to flee or defend itself.

During moult the animal is totally helpless.

During postmoult its sensory structures may be in vibrant renewed contact with the world, but the new exoskeleton is far too soft to allow for any effective defense, being too easily pierced or ruptured.

During all these vulnerable phases the animal seals itself in its burrow as its only means of protection.

If there are any complications during the moulting process the animal may remain trapped in its old exoskeleton to die a slow, lingering death.

LOSS OF LIMB

The appendages of arthropods are constructed like pipes, usually with more or less rigid walls. If a portion of such an appendage is severely damaged or lost, would it not be advantageous to be able to "turn off a valve" a little closer to the body to prevent body fluids from leaking out? If the limb were supplied with a weakened place just outside the "valve" it could even be broken off or lost at this more convenient place. Indeed, if the injured limb were a threat to the animal's survival, the owner might even be provoked into removing it at that special point. And, if it were held by a tenacious predator or caught in a crevice it might be better to lose the limb than to forfeit life!

All of these methods are used by various arthropods in dealing with damaged or incapacitated limbs, and biologists recognize at least four basic categories of limb removal (Savory, 1964): autotomy, autospasy, autotilly, and autophagy.

In general, autotomy refers to the dropping or casting off of a limb through some physiological or anatomical mechanism of the animal, as opposed to a behavioral characteristic. Crustacea (of the other vast wing of the arthropods, the Mandibulata) have a special chitinous edge and muscle arrangement at a particular place *inside* their legs. If the limb is injured severely enough, a physiological or nervous reflex flexes that muscle and causes the limb to be sheared off.

Autospasy means that the limb was removed by some outside force, as by a predator, against the will or contrary to the actions of the owner.

Autotilly usually means that the owner of the limb intentionally removed the injured limb. This is a behavioral mechanism founded either in conscious effort or in instinct.

Autophagy is taken to mean that the animal eats the limb after removing it, a form of autocannibalism! The author would go one step farther and require that the owner of the limb ate it as the sole means of removing it, as opposed to the instance where the limb was eaten after removal.

Not all arthropods exhibit any or all of these characteristics, nor do all arachnids. However, spiders in general, and tarantulas in particular, do have a joint, between the coxa and the trochanter, which has a peculiar arrangement. The coxa has a heavily sclerotized, collarlike ring around its distal end (away from the body) which serves to reinforce it. A pliable hinge membrane connects the trochanter to this coxal ring, but this hinge is somewhat narrowed between the two joints, a little like the interlink spaces in a chain of sausages. It is also weaker than any of the other hinges. Coincidentally, inside the heavy coxal ring there is a circle of soft tissue that is a diaphragm, like the head of a drum with a hole in it, which tends to block off the inner space that runs up the length of the leg.

If enough force is applied anywhere towards the end of the leg this coxa/trochanter hinge is the part that tears first, and the entire leg from that point outwards is cast off. The diaphragm remains across the end of the coxa to act as a block, and a hemolymph clot soon plugs the relatively small hole. Ultimately, only an empty socket remains.

Tarantulas are eminently capable of losing limbs through autotilly and autospasy. There is no provision for them to lose limbs through autotomy; and indeed, autotomy probably does not occur in any arachnid (Wood, 1926).

If pulled hard enough by a predator, a leg will merely separate and drop. In the case of an injured leg, the tarantula may strain to reach around and grasp it with the fangs, pedipalps, or other legs in an effort to remove it. It is nearly always successful. In the case of a damaged terminal segment (e.g., telotarsus), the tip may simply wither and dry. It will be shed during the next moult and be replaced during the moult after that.

REGENERATION

During successive moults the lost limb gradually regenerates. At first it is quite small, though fully formed, but grows with each moult to become full sized in two to four years (Illus. 14 and 15). Other appendages may similarly be regenerated.

A word should be said here about pain in tarantulas. Their anatomies and physiologies are so different that we would be tempted to declare that they do not feel pain in the same sense

Illus. 14. A Haitian tarantula with two missing legs. The right pedipalp, lost more than a year before, has regenerated through one moult.

Illus. 15. This is the same animal shown on the previous page (Illus. 14), but photographed two years later when it was virtually whole and normal again.

that we do, thus giving us a means of assuaging our consciences when we do something that might hurt them. The fact is that they *do* react noticeably to external stimuli that we might call pain, and this has been reported by several researchers.

In the case of autotilly their anatomies are apparently set up so as to shut off the pain sensors when the limb is removed. We may assume that this is the only time that they do not evidence the pain reflex.

ADDENDUM

The fact that so little physiological research has been done on tarantulas is particularly surprising when one considers that tarantulas are fairly representative of all spiders, readily acquired and kept, relatively safe to handle, inexpensive, and large enough to allow technicians to work on them easily.

Tarantulas have an anatomy which is radically different from anything that most of us would call normal. They have a total of eight pairs of appendages while we are only used to two. They have no jaws, but possess highly specialized and efficient weapons instead. They have no distinct "heads" but carry their brains in their "chests." Their stomachs are there too, instead of in an abdomen. While their heart and lungs are toward their rear, the male's intromittent sex organs are up front. Their skeletons are on the outside and their excretory organs bear almost no analogy to ours whatsoever. Upside down, inside out, and backwards, they seem as alien as any animal could be. No wonder they are such prime subjects for myths, old wives' tales, and horror movies.

And yet, the magnitude and scope of these differences are what make these gentle giants of the spider world so fascinating to us.

3

The Scientific
Tarantula

TAXONOMY

Scientists, with their penchant for organization, have developed a system for classifying all living things (Blackwelder, 1963). The basic idea behind this organization is that all modern, living organisms evolved from some prehistoric precursors which in turn evolved from some more ancient ancestors. Thus, a giant "family tree" might be constucted which would clearly illustrate how closely and in what ways each organism was related to every other. This relationship is called the phylogenetic relationship and the method for applying names to its members is called the taxonomic system. This system takes on two functions; not only is it a filing system like a telephone book, it is also a genealogical system like a family tree.

By using such a system it is possible to consider a collection of different kinds of organisms to be remotely related to each other. We may then subdivide them into a hierarchy of succeedingly smaller and more intimately related categories. Ultimately we will be left with a number of more or less distinct kinds of organisms. The members of each individual kind will freely interbreed among themselves, but, for a variety of reasons, normally will not interbreed with the members of other kinds. We will find that the offspring of each interbreeding kind will closely resemble its parents, minor variations being ignored.

Taxonomists—scientists who attempt to determine the phylogenetic relationships between organisms and name them accordingly—use the word "species" to mean the same as "kinds." Incidentally, both the singular and plural forms are "species." These taxonomists define a species as an interbreeding population of organisms whose offspring routinely resemble their parents. The science which deals with this organization and naming is called taxonomy.

There are serious obstacles in the path of perfecting this system. First, we know almost nothing of the ancestors of our modern plants and animals. There are fossils to be sure, but they are seldom complete, showing the whole organism, roots, stems, leaves, flowers, fruit, and seeds; or skeleton, muscle, viscera, genitals, and skin. Second, neither do fossils give us a complete, unbroken record of evolution. There are "missing links" in the record and sometimes entire evolutionary lines, which we are sure existed, left no traces; yet we have their descendants today. Third, there are unsettling shortcomings in the basic theory of evolution. For instance, we have yet to develop a good explanation of the mechanism behind seemingly sudden, massive changes in a line of organisms that had been stable for eons. Similarly, no strong argument defining the mechanism of parallel evolution has been forthcoming.

An alternate theory, Creationism, falls even shorter of explaining all the facts. Either it has not had enough time to deal successfully with the immense size and complexity of the problem or it is basically in error.

We may compare ourselves to a man in a boat over a submerged forest. He can see the tips of the branches of a giant tree and can make out a vague shape through the murky water. He occasionally finds small bits of bark and leaves that float to the surface, but he cannot see enough to reconstruct the whole tree. The taxonomist has an infinitely more formidable task. While our boatman only has several hundred twigs above the water and only a 50- or 100-foot tree beneath, the taxonomist has literally untold millions of species, living and extinct, and an evolutionary history going back perhaps three or more *billion* years. Thus the complexity of the task and the paucity and obscurity of the clues serve to make the project's completion impossible.

Still, all is not hopeless. By carefully examining living organisms and comparing them with obviously related fossil ones, missing parts and even missing links can be constructed. A broad, coarse idea can be built which outlines the basic patterns of evolution when these are compared among several distantly related lines. After these patterns are established, phylogenetic relationships become clearer, a taxonomic system can be formulated, and we can make fairly accurate guesses about the characteristics of any organism by knowing its classification and how it was named. By means of frequent and persistent reexamination and cross-checking of the evidence, as more and more becomes available, most errors can be eliminated from this "boot-strapping" procedure.

In theory the system is fairly simple and straightforward. The major complicating factors are the immense number of organisms and the enormous time spans involved. The major defect is our inability to determine the finer details.

Thus we present the following scheme of classification with the clear understanding that it is tentative, probably in error, and always subject to future revision.

For our purposes we can adopt the admittedly simple-minded point of view that any living thing that is not a plant is an animal. All such animals are then lumped into one huge category: the animal kingdom. This animal kingdom comprises more than 1.2 million species of living organisms and untold millions of extinct ones. It is divided and subdivided through a complex of levels and sublevels. Each such level and division (and therefore group of animals) is called a taxon (plural: taxa).

In the animal kingdom one such principal taxon, called a phylum (Table 1), is composed of all animals having an exoskeleton impregnated with chitin, and with more or less rigid, jointed appendages. This phylum is called Arthropoda—far and away the largest and most successful group of animals on our planet (Meglitch, 1972).

Table 1
PHYLA IN THE ANIMAL KINGDOM

Protozoa	Aschelminthes	Priapuloidea
Mesozoa	Acanthocephela	Arthropoda
Porifera	Ectoprocta	Pentastomida
Coelenterata	Phoronidea	Tardigrada
Ctenophora	Brachiopoda	Chaetognatha
Platyhelminthes	Mollusca	Echinodermata
Gnathostomulida	Annelida	Pogonophora
Nemertinea	Sipunculoidea	Hemichordata
Entoprocta	Echiuroidea	Chordata

One subcategory of the arthropods, distinguished by having chelicerae rather than true jaws, is the subphylum called Chelicerata (Table 2).

Table 2
SUBPHYLA IN THE PHYLUM ARTHROPODA

Onychophora	The "walking worms," *Peripatus*
Trilobita	The trilobites, wholly extinct
Chelicerata	Arthropods without true jaws
Mandibulata	Arthropods with true jaws, includes insects, crustaceans, and others

Those chelicerates which possess only one pair of chelicerae, one pair of pedipalps, and four pairs of walking legs are called arachnids, class Arachnida (Savory, 1977) (Table 3).

Table 3
CLASSES IN THE SUBPHYLUM CHELICERATA

Merostomata   Sea scorpions (extinct) and horseshoe crabs
Pycnogonida   Sea spiders
Arachnida   Spiders, scorpions, mites, ticks, etc.

These arachnids are then further divided into yet smaller subdivisions called orders, one of which is the order Araneae (Table 4)—our spiders. These are characterized by possessing two-segmented chelicerae containing venom glands, a single carapace over the prosoma, and a narrow pedicel separating the prosoma and opisthosoma.

Table 4
ORDERS IN THE CLASS ARACHNIDA

Scorpionida	Scorpions
Pedipalpi	Uropygi (whip scorpions, vinegaroons) and Amblypygi (tailless whip scorpions—genus *Tarantula* belongs here)
Palpigrada	No common name
Araneae	Spiders (also called Araneida)
Solpugida	Sun spiders (also called Solifugae)
Pseudoscorpionida	Pseudoscorpions
Podogona	No common name (also called Ricinuleida)
Phalangida	Harvestmen, "daddy longlegs" (also called Opiliones)
Acarina	Mites and ticks (also called Acari)

The spiders are broken into three suborders (Table 5). One, the Mesothelae, is quite rare and found only in Asia, and is insignificant to us; but the other two are of paramount importance. The division between these last two is based on the attachment, or ar-

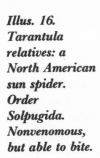

Illus. 16.
Tarantula
relatives: a
North American
sun spider.
Order
Solpugida.
Nonvenomous,
but able to bite.

ticulation, of their chelicerae. If these are attached beneath the spider's "face" and if the fangs work more or less towards each other, like old-fashioned ice tongs (Illus. 17), the animals are considered to be true spiders, suborder Labidognatha. If, on the other hand, the chelicerae are attached to the front of the "face" and work more or less parallel to each other, like your index and middle fingers, they are considered to be the not-so-true spiders called orthognaths, suborder Orthognatha. The differences between these two groups probably are great enough to warrant this division, but there is some criticism over considering orthognaths not to be true spiders. Some older books call these, in order, Liphistiomorphae, Araneomorphae, and Mygalomorphae.

Table 5
SUBORDERS OF THE ORDER ARANEAE

Mesothela	Very primitive, rare spiders (also called Liphistiomorphae)
Orthognatha	Tarantulas and tarantula-like spiders (also called Mygalomorphae)
Labidognatha	Most common spiders (also called Araneomorphae)

***Illus. 17.
Tarantula
relatives: a large
desert wolf
spider. Suborder
Labidognatha.
The eyes are not
on an ocular
tubercle and the
chelicerae are
joined to the
body beneath the
"face."***

The orthognaths, in turn, are composed of several families (Table 6), one of which is the family Theraphosidae—our tarantulas. The theraphosids are further split into genera (singular: genus) such as *Avicularia, Serecopelma* and *Dugesiella*. In each of these genera there may be one or more species. The genus name with the species name (specific epithet) is considered the true name for the animal, for instance *Dugesiella hentzi* (Gerard). The genus name is always capitalized and the genus and species names are always italicized, or underlined if italics aren't possible. If there is a third name in italics a subspecies is indicated. If the last

***Illus. 18.
Tarantula
relatives: a large
Costa Rican
hunting spider.
Suborder
Labidognatha.***

word is a person's name and is not italicized (but may be abbreviated or in parentheses) the person who first described that species—the authority—is indicated.

Table 6
FAMILIES OF THE SUBORDER ORTHOGNATHA

Ctenizidae	Trapdoor spiders
Barychelidae	Trapdoor spiders closely related to the Ctenizidae
Theraphosidae	Tarantulas as defined in this book
Dipluridae	Funnel web spiders
Mecicobothriidae	Funnel web tarantulas very closely related to the Dipluridae
Atypidae	Purse web spiders (the deadly *Atrax* of Australia belongs here)
Antrodiaetidae	The folding door spiders

The classification of one of our common American tarantulas might appear like this:

Kingdom	Animalia
Phylum	Arthropoda
Subphylum	Chelicerata
Class	Arachnida
Order	Araneae
Suborder	Orthognatha
Family	Theraphosidae
Genus	*Dugesiella*
Species	*hentzi*
Authority	(Gerard)

Of course we don't give this entire scheme every time we wish to discuss this animal. In the interest of saving time and space we assume that the reader has some familiarity with the general

Illus. 19.
Tarantula
relatives: a
trapdoor spider
from Texas.
Family
Ctenizidae.

scheme of classification or knows enough to be able to look it up in the appropriate reference book. At the beginning of a scientific paper the class or order and family names are normally given to help the reader locate himself among the bewildering legions of animals. At the same time the authority's name should also be given. Thereafter only the scientific name or its abbreviation (e.g., *D. hentzi*) need be used. While this custom should also be used in nonscientific papers it is not often adhered to.

The spider from which our tarantulas borrowed their names is classified among the "true" spiders (Labidognatha) and is a wolf spider (family Lycosidae) called *Lycosa tarantula* (Rossi). Black widow spiders and their relatives are also true spiders in the family Theridiidae. The most notorious one is *Lactrodactus mactans* (Fabricius) (see Color Illus. Q).

Does this sound like a needlessly complex system? Try counting to one million. At one count per second, forty hours per week, you will require nearly seven weeks! And, the order in your counting is already determined because you already know that five follows four, six follows five, and so on. You don't have to discover or devise a system for keeping your "creatures" in some order. Now perhaps you begin to appreciate the problem. You must also remember that there are literally millions more animals that once lived and are now extinct but must still be worked into the system.

Now a word of caution: In this book we are more or less equating the term "tarantula" with the family Theraphosidae. The reader is cautioned against accepting this as being completely correct. There are some theraphosids which we might not consider as tarantulas, and there are some spiders from closely allied families that we might consider to be tarantulas. There are many people in this world who apply the name to *any* large spider, and the taxonomist accepts the term *Tarantula* to mean a member of a distantly related group of arachnids which aren't even spiders!

The taxonomic system outlined was developed to uniquely describe each living or extinct organism. A complementary system was also developed to allow for organized name changes when they became necessary for some reason. Theoretically this would allow someone to "track" through the name changes in a logical order. The ultimate intention of this was to avoid the immense amount of confusion described in the previous paragraph. As we shall see shortly, precisely the reverse is true where theraphosids are concerned.

IDENTIFICATION

Here is where all that grand organization falls apart. The theraphosids are a very difficult group to subcategorize, name, and identify.

Because their ancestors were soft-bodied they left almost no fossil record of their origin and evolution. Their kind appears as suddenly out of the mists of time as they themselves do out of the dark on a warm desert evening (Savory, 1964). In fact, the earliest known fossil orthognath (mygalomorph) spider only dates from some 60 million years ago, about the same time that the dinosaurs became extinct. By contrast, the earliest known spider, a mesothele (liphistiomorph), dates from about 360 million years ago, about *six* times older! Yet, the general consensus of opinion holds that orthognaths are "primitive" spiders and probably existed for some time before that earliest known fossil. This is an example of an evolutionary line that we are certain existed, but left no traces.

Because we have so little fossil evidence to help us define the various species' relationships we must rely on their physical characteristics alone, and they have few obviously definitive characters that can be used to categorize them. Pigmentation and patterns are too untrustworthy to be used as anything but the most superficial guide. Closely related species might not resemble each other in the slightest, and unrelated species frequently mimic each other (see Color Illus. H and K). Furthermore, the best method of identifying a tarantula is to compare it to the original specimen which was preserved in alcohol or formaldehyde. But, such specimens rapidly fade, turning to various shades of drab tan and brown.

Virtually all tarantulas are constructed alike. They all have the same number of legs, the same number of leg segments, the same eye arrangement, the same number and arrangement of spinnerets. In nearly all cases the difference between the sexes is greater than the difference between the species (see Color Illus. F and G). Because of this, several species were inadvertently given separate names for each sex by early investigators (Roewer, 1942–1954).

Therefore, a large portion of our problem involves *finding* distinguishing characters on which to base a description and identification.

The second major obstacle is to determine which of those characters are significant and which are trivial. The taxonomist attempts to lump together closely related groups and to separate those which he feels are not closely related. But what does he use to distinguish these affinities? Leg length? Fang size? Venom chemistry? Odor? Pigmentation? One attempt which shows promise uses the characteristics of the hair from the top of the opisthosoma, the urticating bristles (Cook, et al, 1972).

At this time the state of the art can best be called chaotic. There is no definitive work yet published which neatly categorizes all, or even a large portion of, the known tarantulas. Herein lies our failing. The only ways that we have of identifying a given tarantula are the following:

1. Compare it to named specimens in collections at major museums, if we are allowed near them in the first place.
2. Compare it to written descriptions, often in foreign languages or in obscure scientific journals, which we laboriously unearth in major libraries.
3. Send cast skins or preserved specimens to recognized authorities for identification, then often wait months to find that they can't identify it because our material was inadequate or reference specimens are unavailable.
4. Try to find lists or keys to the fauna of the area in which the tarantula was collected, if this is known, and hope that the key or list is correct.

Furthermore, many descriptions date from as far back as the late eighteenth century and are nearly impossible to find. Since that time, classification has changed radically. During the fifty years between 1913 and 1963 there were no less than sixteen attempts to reorganize the arachnids as a whole into a coherent system (Savory, 1964). Not one of these attempts has proven completely successful. During all this confusion many theraphosids were inadvertently misnamed or named twice. Indeed, the very concept of "species" has changed radically since that time and if current definitions were universally applied we may safely assume that there would occur yet another upheaval in classification. Even then there is serious doubt that our current scheme of phylogenetic relationships is correct (Cook, et al, 1972), thus introducing yet *another* reorganization with its attendant confusion.

The bottom line is this: The taxonomy, classification, and identification of theraphosids may be at least one hundred, and perhaps two hundred, years out of date. During that time numerous important advances were not applied to the group or were applied only haphazardly and incompletely. At this point perhaps the single greatest need is for one or more competent arachnologists to take on the task of sorting out the mess. The field is wide open and waiting for anyone with the interest and qualifications to accept the challenge. While the researcher will not become overabundantly wealthy, he will discover fame and much gratitude from those of us who wander around with flashlights seeking dark, eight-legged shapes with glowing eyes in the still, desert night.

4

The Wild
Tarantula

DISTRIBUTION

Tarantulas are found on every continent that has warm-temperate to tropical climates, except perhaps Europe (Illus. 20).

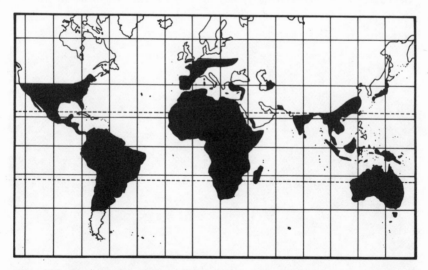

Illus. 20. Distribution of the Orthognatha. This illustrates how widely tarantulas and tarantulalike spiders are spread around the world. (After Savory, 1964.)

(No wonder the amazement of Renaissance explorers!) They are found in a broad belt around the earth in nearly every type of habitat, from subalpine to rain forest to desert (Gertsch, 1979). Some are arboreal (Cook, 1972), most are terrestrial, none are aquatic or marine.

Little is known of the lifestyles of most of them. We can only assume that they parallel those of our more thoroughly studied North American species and try to imagine adjustments for differences in seasons, temperature, moisture, and habitat. Be forewarned! These assumptions will surely lead us astray. The theraphosids have been around too long to fit neatly into any prescribed formula. Surprises await us, and our prejudices are to be used only as a starting point. Far more field research is desperately needed.

THE HUMBLE ABODE

Most tarantulas seem to prefer relatively dry areas, though not necessarily deserts (Illus. 21). For instance, a common North

Illus. 21. Tarantula terrain! This Texas chaparral was dotted with literally hundreds of tarantula burrows.

Illus. 22. This tarantula burrow yielded a "Rio Grande gold." Frequently the burrows are covered with a thin veil-like web indicating that someone is indeed home.

American species lives on well-drained hillsides in areas of firm soil and sparse grasses in Arkansas (Baerg, 1958). Their domiciles are usually unbranched burrows one or more feet deep and as much as an inch or inch-and-a-half in diameter. While they may be dug under stones or grass hummocks, more usually they occur merely in the open—distributed more or less at random (Illus. 22). The diameter of the burrow may enlarge somewhat just inside the mouth to suggest a chamber, though a definite atrium is seldom found. The bottom end of the burrow usually expands slightly to produce a small chamber which serves as the animal's *sanctum sanctorum*. This bottom chamber frequently is dug at an angle to the axis of the main shaft, so that the floor may be nearly horizontal. However, if the ground is rocky the burrow may be twisted and contorted with no such enlargements or chambers readily evident.

The author has found small leaves, remains of eaten prey, and the remnants of cast skins on the floors of these chambers. The burrows may be lined with silk, but more commonly are not. We do not yet know the reason for the variation. Will a tarantula move into an empty, preexisting burrow? How many burrows does a tarantula dig during its life? Do tarantulas ever engage in contests over possession of the same burrow? No answers are available to any of these questions.

When the animal is resting, the burrow's mouth may be covered with a thin, almost invisible veil of silk. When the animal is active the veil is gone and the mouth of the burrow is sometimes surrounded with an area of silken threads laid down as "drag lines" to help the tarantula find its home again. If a beetle should scurry through this area, the tarantula might be lucky enough to catch it, though the web is never used as a snare. Neither is the web ever suspended between two objects in the same fashion as the webs of the more advanced orb-weaving spiders. During very

Illus. 23. Leg I on a male tarantula showing the femoral hook.

cold weather the tarantula might plug the entrance with soil or other debris and, being poikilothermic (cold-blooded), lapse into a state of semidormancy, though tarantulas apparently do not hibernate (Baerg, 1958).

Juvenile and female tarantulas may be found singly or in loose aggregations called colonies. This is not to imply purposeful cooperation or gregariousness as practiced by termites and ants. Tarantulas would readily cannibalize each other if given the opportunity. Either they have such limited senses that they simply are unaware that other clan members are near, or they are such timid, retiring creatures that they seldom, if ever, travel far enough to find their neighbors. The colonies apparently are purely accidental. The members seldom move more than a few inches, or at most feet, from their burrows; and when they do they lay down those draglines of silk to help them find their way back.

LIFE CYCLE

The moult which occurs during a tarantula's tenth, eleventh, or twelfth year is a particularly significant one. This moult is the animal's maturing moult. The exact year may depend on the species, the individual animal's physical condition, or some other, unknown factor.

Before this moult all tarantulas of the same species appear more or less alike, and after it the mature female still appears and acts like a large juvenile.

The male, however, undergoes a radical transformation during his maturing moult (see Color Illus. F and G). He develops longer legs and a smaller body than his sisters, and his first pair of legs now bears prominent hooks on each femur, pointing forward (Illus. 23). His personality has also changed. Instead of the sedate, reclusive demeanor of a female, he has adopted a very excitable, nervous personality characterized by impetuous starts, quick flights, and a strong wanderlust. One of the most important changes occurs in his pedipalps. While his sister's pedipalps still resemble walking legs his appear like boxing gloves. But do not be mistaken, he's a lover, not a fighter! The bulbous ends of his pedipalps are intricately adapted for use as very specialized sex organs.

We know very little about the natural sex lives of wild tarantulas. Virtually all we do know arises from captive specimens, and life in captivity can radically alter habits and instincts. Witness the fact that interspecific hybrids among animals are almost unheard of in the wild, while common in captivity. Examples are mules (horse × ass) and "red factor" canaries (common canary × red siskin finch). We will assume here that captive and wild habit patterns are identical, as indeed they are in most cases, and leave the contradictions to subsequent investigators.

Shortly after the maturing moult the male tarantula may spin a sperm web (Baerg, 1928 and 1958; Minch, 1979; Petrunkevitch, 1911). This is a lean-to style silken tent with at least two openings separated by a narrow "bridge." He will climb under it and, upside down, deposit a droplet of semen, containing his sperm, on the underside of the bridge. After climbing back up on top of the web he will reach with his pedipalps, first one and then the other, and fill them with semen. The clubbed end of the pedipalp is a marvelous instrument, reminiscent of an exotic wine bottle with a long twisted neck (Illus. 24). Normally the neck, or embolus (plural: emboli), is folded back against the rest of the pedipalp, out of harm's way. But, when the body of the flask, or bulb, is being filled with semen, and later when it is being used to impregnate a female, it is unfolded so that the embolus is fully exposed. After loading his pedipalps he destroys the web and "goes a-courtin'."

The hyperactivity of the male is a survival characteristic. During the courting phase of his life he wanders freely, searching for females. Merely hiding during the light of day, he no longer maintains a permanent home, while the fair damsels he seeks normally stay home waiting for their suitors. During his wanderings the male is fair game for any predators in the area, and he must be hyperactive merely to survive and breed. Of course, the more ground he covers the better are his chances of finding a female, and males have been known to wander many miles.

When he finds a female he approaches her warily. If the female

Illus. 24. Pedipalp of a male tarantula showing the bulb and embolus.

remains quiescent he may touch her with the tips of his first pair of legs, or tap the ground, or tap her several times. There may be a brief pause, then he'll twitch his legs. He may alternate these displays repeatedly until he is convinced that the female means him no harm. If she is still passive he will move closer, sliding his front legs up between her pedipalps and up over her "face." At the same time she will rear up and extend her fangs. This brings his femoral hooks into direct contact with them. He locks her fangs with his hooks, to steady both himself and the female, and perhaps out of self-defense, and pushes her prosoma up and backwards. She bends sharply at the pedicel. At this point he reaches under her with one pedipalp, unfolds the embolus, and carefully inserts it into the genital opening on her epigastric furrow. After emptying one pedipalp he inserts and empties the other. Thus, the semen is deposited into two small chambers, spermathecae (singular: spermathecum), just inside her genital openings.

Does the male have to build a new sperm web and "reload" between matings, or can he successfully impregnate more than one female from each "loading"? We don't know.

The actual sequence of events and the exact amount and type of foreplay may differ with each species and may hold important clues to their phylogenetic relationships (Platnick, 1971). No one has yet made a serious study of this phenomenon in tarantulas.

After copulation (mating) the male holds the female as far away as possible until he can safely unhook his front legs and run! The female frequently chases him a short distance but seldom catches him. She is one of the predators that he must outrun, but our lover nearly always lives to seduce another maiden.

Within a few months after maturing the male dies of old age. Seldom do our North American species live through the winter, almost never beyond spring (Baerg, 1958). At this time no data are available on the exotic species, although the author once had a male "Mexican red leg" that survived some fourteen months or more after his maturing moult. Unfortunately, no precise dates were kept so no exact time limits could be established. Without question, older, failing males become easy prey and therefore would have a much shorter life expectancy in the wild.

The author has collected numerous males in south Texas as late in the spring as the first of June. While most were evidently survivors from the previous fall, judging from their general appearance, a small but significant proportion (perhaps one in five or six) neither appeared emaciated nor showed signs of physical damage or bristle loss. This would suggest that they had moulted that spring rather than the previous fall. From this we may draw two assumptions: First, that in warmer regions more males survive the winter than may be thought; second, that a significant number of males actually go through the maturing moult in early spring and it is possible that they then copulate with the females in time for the summer egg laying. Thus, the mating season may not be as restricted as was once thought (Baerg, 1928, 1958; Minch, 1978).

The female will over-winter in her burrow. The semen which the male transferred to her is carefully harbored in her spermathecae until the following spring. In June or July she will spin a walnut-sized, cocoonlike ootheca (egg case) holding up to 1,000 or more eggs. She will tend it carefully, airing it at the burrow's entrance and protecting it. She can become quite aggressive while guarding it.

We are not certain of the incubation time for the eggs of most species, but it undoubtedly varies somewhat with the weather. One common North American species of tarantula spiderlings emerges from the ootheca in August and usually leaves the mother's burrow a week or so later to fend for themselves (Baerg, 1958). There is no parental care as there is among scorpions. Shortly after the young ones leave home the female will moult and, along with the rest of the exoskeleton, the linings of the spermathecae and any extra semen they still hold will be cast off. Our lady will again be a virgin.

If she didn't mate in time to lay fertile eggs the female will moult somewhat earlier, July rather than September.

Newly emerged spiderlings measure only about one-sixth inch in length and are light brown with a prominent black patch on their opisthosomas (Illus. 25). These are the urticating bristles

Illus. 25. A juvenile "southwestern brown" tarantula with a conspicuous patch of urticating bristles.

that they will need for self-defense. After leaving their mother's burrow, baby tarantulas are seldom found until they are almost half grown. We know little of this early period in their lives except that the rate of mortality must be enormous.

In the course of flooding tarantulas from their burrows the author has noted large populations of springtails, minute primitive insects of the order Collembola, living as commensals in the burrows. These could serve as the spiderlings' secondary food, next after their siblings.

The prairie and chaparral regions where tarantulas are common also hold large populations of termites. While baby tarantulas have never been reported to eat them in the wild we know of no reason why they couldn't, except for the termites' presumed inaccessability. Perhaps termites also serve as an important source of "baby food."

In addition, while excavating the adults' burrows, the author found neighboring burrows, some eight inches in length and less than one-quarter inch in diameter, with baby tarantulas at the bottom. These spiderlings had a leg span of less than one-half inch. On occasion, these smaller burrows are more numerous than the adults' burrows. One must merely look for them more carefully.

According to Baerg (1958) the greatest menace to the eggs and newly hatched spiderlings is ants. The adult, brooding female will abandon its ootheca almost immediately if confronted by marauding ants. These ants can then proceed to tear open the silken case and consume the eggs or baby tarantulas with complete impunity. Apparently ants do not normally bother adult or juvenile tarantulas.

In captivity, baby tarantulas moult quite frequently, as often as four or five times a year (Baerg, 1938). By their seventh year they are nearly full grown and the black patch has expanded to cover their entire opisthosoma.

It is almost impossible to determine the sex of a juvenile tarantula as there are no obvious secondary sexual characteristics. There may be a slight difference in the size of the chelicerae compared to the prosoma, with the prospective male's chelicerae and fangs being smaller than the female's, but the differences are subtle. Juvenile males who are approaching their maturing moult may exhibit a slight change in personality (tending towards the male hyperactivity), but this is far more obvious in retrospect than in foresight.

A female may live a total of 25 years or more (Baerg, 1963). However, as old age approaches she will miss occasional moults and eventually die. She has few enemies. She is difficult to attack in her burrow, and she is larger and more powerful than most other predaceous arthropods, the only significant exception being the tarantula hawk wasp. Coyotes, coati-mundies, opossums, armadillos, and mice may occasionally try to eat tarantulas, but normally hunt other prey. Once exposed to a face full of those irritating bristles further contacts are avoided unless driven by starvation. In fact, mice that were tested were found to have died from the irritation to their mucous membranes (Cook, et al, 1972).

A word should be said about the famed tarantula hawk wasp, although a thorough discussion is beyond the scope of this book. Briefly, these wasps are classified in the genera *Pepsis* and *Hemipepsis* (order Hymenoptera, family Pompilidae) and are notorious for using stung, incapacitated (though still live) tarantulas as food for their developing larvae. The details of their technique and the apparent nonchalance of the tarantula when confronted by one of them is very interesting. However, while the phenomenon may be remarkable, it is by no means unique as there are many smaller wasps the world over which routinely prey on spiders in a similar fashion. Indeed, this seems to be typical for several families of wasps. In the broad overview the only really remarkable aspect of the hawk wasp versus tarantula relationship is their great size, and this characteristic has made them particularly vulnerable to exploitation by sensationalists. Thus the erroneous impression is generated that these animals are somehow unusual or unique. (For more information, refer to Petrunkevitch, 1926 and 1952; and William, 1956.)

ENDANGERED SPECIES

A major problem with tarantulas is the great length of their life cycles. Once a colony is seriously molested it will require years, perhaps decades, to recover, if ever. The result is that these gentle giants, of which we know so little, could be in danger of extinction before we have a chance to study them.

In many locales tarantulas appear quite numerous and in little danger. However, this impression may be based on the layman's casual observation of wandering males. These observations are imprecise and open to question on several counts. First, little or no attempt was made to keep an accurate count of the number of individuals sighted, and the unenlightened are sure to exaggerate the numbers for the sake of drama. Second, no attempt was made to identify the species sighted, thus we have no good qualitative data. Third, the males are notorious for wandering many miles, thus the exact position of the colony is still unknown. Fourth, no collaborative data exist which would indicate which species are common and which are rare, threatened, or endangered in any given area.

For the nominal species of North America (variously estimated from 12 to 40) there are no accurate maps or range records to give any sort of distribution data, and we certainly have no real idea of how common or rare any species really is. Thus, without rigorous scientific data the abundance of one species may mask the peril of another. While a major disturbance of one of their colonies may have little overall effect to the common species, it could wipe out a rare one.

One such disturbance is depredation by man. The pet industry is responsible for the capture of literally thousands of tarantulas per year (Browning, 1981). If this collecting is done with some wisdom the wild populations can easily survive. We have learned to harvest and manage deer, waterfowl, and fish populations, for example, to actually increase their numbers. The same might be possible with selected populations of tarantulas. The tragedy of the situation is that the collectors are usually unenlightened natives who, because they are living at the poverty level, are interested only in their immediate monetary gain. The matter is compounded by the simple fact that no one but those collectors knows where the collection sites are and we have no way of assessing the plight of the colonies. Please do not take this as a condemnation of the pet industry. That industry is perhaps one of the few real hopes for survival that many small animals have in the face of civilization's onslaught. Rather, the point is that a problem *may* exist but not enough is known about these animals to allow for a balanced, rational plan of action.

A far more menacing threat is civilization itself. No animal on earth is capable of surviving an army of bulldozers. Tarantulas are no exception. Realistically, no suburbanite or apartment-dweller is going to willingly cohabit with a colony of giant hairy spiders (in spite of this book); and tarantulas would find the task of setting up housekeeping in a shopping-center parking lot impossible. Furthermore, the reckless abandon that man displays in spraying his environment with pesticides is nothing short of criminal. The end result is that the tarantula, as well as many other innocuous animals, may be in dire straits before we can do anything about it.

Perhaps the most practical solution would be a three-pronged management effort. First, fund the necessary research to develop the data needed for intelligent decision making. Second, identify colonies of remarkable character and establish preserves to protect them. These could easily be made compatible with other wildlife interests. Third, prohibit or severely curtail the collecting of tarantulas from those areas where unique or rare species are found. From those areas where tarantulas are plentiful, collection quotas should be established to allow limited exploitation without seriously endangering the wild population. Thus, private industry could maintain its market, you could still get your pets, and the best interests of the animals would still be protected.

The hobbyist can have a significant part in this. First, by actively seeking the appropriate legislation he can help ensure a continued supply of pets for his hobby while still protecting a valuable form of wildlife. Second, a concerted effort should be made by the hobbyist to discover the techniques and "tricks" required to breed these animals in captivity. Hopefully, a captive breeding population of the rarer species would remove the pressures of collection from the wild populations. More than one species of animal has been saved from extinction by this method.

Over and above everything else, one thing must be understood: Absolutely the last thing needed is a band of wild-eyed pseudo-ecologists or animal protectionists brandishing placards and railroading the government into ill-advised, poorly conceived, and incompetently implemented panic legislation. First we need *facts* and hard *data.* Then we need *careful* action. All wildlife (including tarantulas) is threatened enough as it is!

5

The Pet
Tarantula

RATIONALE

Before attempting to discuss the care of tarantulas we must first ask ourselves why anyone would want to keep a pet tarantula. The following is a sample of some of the reasons that were actually given.

1. Status symbol. (Act now! Be the *first* on your block!)
2. Keeps mother (wife) out of your room (workshop).
3. Conversation piece. (Not necessarily limited to "EEK! A SPIDER!")
4. Satisfies a need to keep a pet when your lease says "NO PETS," so you hide it in a bureau drawer.
5. Simple curiosity. They *are* different.
6. Scientific study. ("Well, actually I'm doing research on horror flicks . . . .")
7. Your nephew bought one and his mother won't let him keep it in the house. So, you (you poor gullible fool!) consented to keep it for him and let him see it every Saturday. Now you find out that they live 20 years!

8. You really hate your roommate, so you hope its bite is lethal. (Attack, Morte! Kill!)
9. Somebody told you that they make good pets (no hair on the carpet, no litters every four months, etc.) so you got one. And you know? They were right!

No doubt you can add to the list. Ultimately, after overcoming your initial apprehensions, you will be even harder pressed to answer: Why not?

MAINTENANCE

Caring for a tarantula is not a very complicated task. Their requirements are simple and undemanding. After the initial briefing it reduces to not doing anything to harm them. Because they are so different it is sometimes hard to perceive their Achilles' heels; and we may do something stupid and lose a valuable pet. So, most of what follows is a list of "DON'TS" to help protect your tarantula. You still must pay close attention to the "DO'S," though.

As a very first point: Tarantulas are antisocial. Keeping more than one per cage almost guarantees that you will end up with only one very fat tarantula. They *are* cannibalistic. With solid dividers you may be able to partition a larger cage to hold several, but they must not be allowed to climb over, knock down, dig under, or squeeze around the barriers. Much safer is a strict "one-tarantula-per-cage" rule.

Cages. The cage can be almost any container that will prevent the escape of the animal or its food. The width should be at least twice as large as the tarantula's maximum leg-span, and the length at least twice as large as the width. The height of the cage should be large enough to allow the animal room to turn over and right itself easily during moulting. This would probably be at least three inches for the average adult. The cage should not be too tall because occasionally tarantulas do climb. In fact, they are surprisingly good at climbing glass! But, because they are such clumsy climbers, they also fall, and any appreciable drop will kill them. As a rule of thumb, the cage should never be more than ten or twelve inches tall, but that is subject to your own judgment.

Many different kinds of cages have been tried with limited success. Squat two-gallon goldfish bowls are inexpensive and have the required floor space, but they are difficult to escape proof and the glass is not clear enough to make them ideal.

Wire, screen, or meshwork cages may be made at home from scrap materials, but they may allow the tarantula's food to escape. In addition, if the tarantula climbs up the sides it could fall and injure itself. If the strands of wire are not welded together (as in hot-dipped galvanized mesh) the animal could catch a claw between two strands. This could result in the loss of the claw or even a leg.

Wooden cages are acceptable providing they are not constructed of cedar. The woods which come from any of the so-called red cedars (actually various species of juniper) contain an aromatic oil—oil of cedar—which is very toxic to most living organisms, especially arthropods. This is the reason for using cedar in the construction of closets and chests. It prevents clothes moth and dermestid beetle infestations. Unfortunately, it is also dangerous to tarantulas. Never keep your pet tarantula in any container that has a cedar smell. Never keep your tarantula's cage on or near a cedar chest or closet.

Never use the absorbent cedar chips (sold as rodent bedding in pet shops) in your tarantula's cage.

Cigar boxes are definitely not acceptable. If they have indeed contained any tobacco products it is almost certain that they are contaminated with nicotine. Nicotine is one of the most potent insecticides known—natural, organic, and deadly! And tarantulas are most definitely *not* immune to it.

Painting or varnishing a wooden cage is recommended. This seals the pores of the wood, making it easier to clean. Be certain that the paint is marked "non-toxic when dry." A semigloss or satin finish is recommended, as the flat finishes are almost as difficult to keep clean as the bare wood, and the high-gloss finishes are too "hard" or harsh appearing in a small cage. Lacquer and shellacs are too fragile to be serviceable in these circumstances.

The major drawback to wooden cages is that you are unable to see into them without opening them, thus risking the escape of your pet. It would be possible to install a glass or plastic window but the trouble might not be worth the effort, even if you did possess the expertise and tools.

Perhaps the ideal cage is an aquarium (Illus. 26). A two- to five-gallon capacity is adequate, a ten-gallon capacity is more than ample. Their convenient rectangular shape fits most decors and they are easily escape proofed. Various styles of screen or wire lids are manufactured specifically to fit the standard sizes, or you can make your own. They are also readily available at pet shops. The currently popular style, made of panes of glass held together with a silicone plastic, and with no metal frames, is lightweight and easily handled. Furthermore, it is easily repaired if one pane is broken. However, they are so inexpensive in the smaller sizes

Illus. 26. Tarantula and cage. The plant is a plastic aquarium decoration. While this may seem to be a rather austere arrangement, it simplifies cleaning and allows the tarantula to be seen and handled easily. Note the water dish at left.

that if more than one pane is broken it is generally less trouble and expense to replace the whole aquarium than to repair it. Hobbyists often make their own all-glass aquaria, but unless the glass is virtually free it is still less expensive to buy the smaller sizes. A word of warning: Use only that silicone plastic which is specifically intended for aquaria. Most others contain a mildew-cide which is extremely toxic.

Whatever cage and escape-proof lid you select should be free of sharp points and edges, inside and out, both for your safety and that of your pet. A secure, absolutely escape-proof top is a necessity. Trying to save money by slighting this last rule is guaranteed to lose your pet.

Substrate. The use of soil as a substrate or bedding by the hobbyist is not recommended here. It tends to absorb and hold moisture and wastes, thus serving to enhance the probability of mould and mite infestations, a factor whose importance we cannot assess as yet. If soil is used it should be steam-sterilized potting soil from a florist or garden shop. One possible use for soil would be as an experimental tool to determine the burrowing habits of your pets (Lund, 1977), but the cage must be kept well ventilated to prevent the build-up of moisture. But such an arrangement would make it almost impossible to handle your pet without tearing up the entire cage.

Practical experience has demonstrated that pet tarantulas can get along quite nicely without burrows, so, for the beginner, we recommend against caging arrangements which allow for them. After you have kept several tarantulas for a year or more and have some experience with their care, you may wish to set up such a cage for the sake of experiment.

As a novice you are better advised to use aquarium gravel from a pet shop. Buy enough to make a layer one-half to one inch thick. This is normally about two and one-half pounds per gallon capacity if you are using one of the common sizes of aquaria. Rinse it with room-temperature tap water and allow it to drain thoroughly before putting it in the cage. Don't worry about the moisture as long as it will evaporate in one or two days. Fine sand (blasting silica) is not recommended on the cage floor because it absorbs and holds moisture indefinitely, quickly turning sour. Very coarse pebbles are difficult for the spider to crawl over, and they allow spaces for bits of food and waste to sift into and mould. Beach sand, even from freshwater shores, is not recommended because it is too fine and may contain harmful concentrations of salts.

Once again, never use cedar shavings. The oil of cedar is definitely toxic.

Newspapers are also questionable. If the ink is old-fashioned lamp black and mineral oil, it might be safe. But if it is derived from coal-tar dyes, it is probably toxic.

Also, several years go evidence was found that a chemical in paper derived from fir trees resembled some of the hormones in insects which stop their maturation (Slama and Williams, 1966). It was suggested that virtually all paper manufactured in the United States possessed this substance. No one has shown a similar effect in tarantulas, but that is probably due to the fact that no one has looked. You should not take the chance with your valuable pets. However, if you do manage to get your tarantulas to breed, you might separate a few of the spiderlings from the rest and keep them on paper towels or newsprint to compare their rates of development and maturation with those which are kept on various other substrates.

Water. You *must* include a water dish in the cage. Even desert tarantulas must be able to drink in captivity. Without the protection of a burrow tarantulas lose water faster than they can acquire it from their food (Cloudsley-Thompson, 1967). The water dish should be wide and shallow enough to allow your pet to straddle or wade into it. It must be able to immerse the entire lower surface of its prosoma in order to drink. Some ashtrays and plastic jar lids are excellent for this purpose, as are petri dishes. The water should be changed at least once a week, whether you see the tarantula drink or not. If you have trouble with your pet's food (usually crickets) drowning in the water dish you can put a small chip of slate in the dish, leaning it against one edge as a ramp. A small pebble will also work but you must be certain to use a large enough water dish to allow your tarantula plenty of room to drink around the pebble.

Cages for Tropical Species. Mounting experience with tropical rain forest species of tarantulas suggests that they may have lost (or failed to acquire) the water-retaining properties of those other species that come from more arid habitats. As a result, dessication is suspected to be a major cause of death in captive rain forest species. At the time of this writing the only such species commonly found in the pet trade is the so-called orange-tipped or pink-toed tarantula. However, it is nearly certain that other rain forest species will be imported from time to time. It is suggested that any tarantula which is suspected of being arboreal (because it persists in resting or constructing a web retreat in the top of its cage) or a rain forest species (because of avowed origin or reasonably reliable identification by an "expert") be kept in a tropical terrarium situation with somewhat higher humidity.

For such cages a leak-free aquarium would be an absolute necessity. Bottle terrariums are impossible because of the difficulty of removing the tarantula without killing it. The terrarium may be planted with *small* tropical plants. For the plants, a light is a necessity but it can *only* be fluorescent. Incandescent bulbs, even in very small wattages, will overheat the terrarium and kill the tarantula, and even a little sunlight will accomplish the same feat, only faster!

At least one half of the top of such a terrarium *must* be open for ventilation and to help prevent the humidity from getting too high. These conditions pose a serious threat of fungus outbreaks and mite infestations. This subject is covered more fully later in this chapter.

The plants in such a terrarium will have to be trimmed back or replaced frequently or they will grow into such an impenetrable tangle that you won't be able to see your pet. Even then, you should not give your pet a place to hide unless you never care to see it again!

Lastly, it is best not to try to keep other pets with the tarantula. American chameleons and other small lizards will only make good (though expensive) food for the spider, and larger lizards will eat it. Some millipedes are notorious for exhaling traces of cyanide gas, and will eat unsightly holes in the plants. Land snails will also eat holes in the plants as well as leave unsightly trails of slime all over. Centipedes have a very toxic bite. Land hermit crabs will tear up the terrarium arrangement like a wrecking crew *and* eat the tarantula!

For the sake of emphasis: DON'T use a bottle terrarium. DON'T use an incandescent light. DON'T place the terrarium anywhere near sunlight. DON'T obstruct more than 50% of the top ventilation of the terrarium. DON'T use such a terrarium without an escape-proof lid. DON'T try to keep other pets with your tarantula.

General Environment. When tarantulas are first received in shipment they usually have a very shrivelled opisthosoma. This is a sign of extreme dehydration. Such animals must be given water immediately and then kept two or three days in a moist container. After regaining their strength they should be offered food as soon as possible. After several days they will begin to appear "normal" and should be moved to their permanent, drier quarters.

On several occasions, during very hot weather, one hobbyist's tarantula was witnessed to submerge itself in a water dish for several hours. At this time no evidence exists to indicate that this may be common practice, but that may be the result of no one bothering to report it. You may experiment by supplying a large enough container of water to allow submersion, but definitely do not force your pet into it.

Any decorations in the cage are largely for the hobbyist. The tarantulas don't seem to care, but then how could you tell? Avoid sharp or pointed ornaments and never use a cactus. Startled pet tarantulas have been known to impale themselves on long cactus spines.

Tarantulas can withstand nearly any temperature that you can. Care should be exercised, however, not to shut them into a stiflingly hot room. Be sure to allow them good ventilation. During the hottest times of the year they should be moved to the coolest room of the building. During the cooler months you may turn the thermostat on your home heating unit down to 60° F. (16° C.) at night without fear as long as you turn it up to 70° F. (21° C.) during the day. Because of the lower night temperature your pet won't eat as much as usual, but you will still have to be very careful to keep fresh water in the cage at all times. Temperatures lower than this may be harmful to tropical species, but those which come from the American Southwest can tolerate temperatures somewhat lower with few, if any, ill effects.

You must be very careful about exposing your tarantula to bright lights or sunlight. At the very least, the animals abhor bright light. Far more important, however, is the accompanying heat. If they are exposed to direct sunlight or trapped in a container (even as big as a car) that is exposed to it they overheat and die very quickly. Don't even allow their cage to sit *near* a sunny window. They don't benefit from the light and the heat can be fatal.

Food. Tarantulas are strict carnivores. They have never been observed to eat anything except meat in one form or another. Because they have such limited senses they usually detect their food by touch, only occasionally by sight. Thus, they eat anything that moves and is small enough to subdue. Photographs exist showing tarantulas eating small lizards and snakes (Caras, 1974). Some of the larger tropical species have a reputation for eating small birds (Butler and Main, 1961), whence "bird spiders" and *"Avicularia,"* but to what extent is still unproven.

Occasionally, hobbyists may feed them newly born mice (pinkies), but mice that are old enough to open their eyes or are already growing fur should be avoided as being dangerously large. During the warmer months they may be fed wild insects from a field or garden that hasn't been exposed to pesticides. The exceptions to this rule are ants, bees, and wasps because of their weaponry. Other really large insects like lubber grasshoppers and stag beetles should also be avoided because they can harm the tarantula as they struggle. Do not risk your valuable pet in combat.

The staple diet in captivity is crickets and mealworms. Both may be purchased from fishing bait dealers and pet shops. The crickets are accepted readily because of their movement, but mealworms will be taken if the tarantula is placed in a shallow dish containing them, and left alone. The mealworms will eventually become black beetles if not eaten. These are also good food, even if a little hard.

The crickets may be allowed to run at liberty in the tarantula's cage as long as a small dish of dry oatmeal or dry dog food is supplied for them to eat. On more than one occasion a tarantula has been nibbled by hungry crickets. The mealworms will burrow out of sight if allowed their freedom. Keep them in the cage with your tarantula in a shallow, flat, dry dish similar to the water dish. A little dry oatmeal or bran cereal should be put in the dish for the mealworms to eat, or they'll starve to death. An alternative is to place the tarantula and the mealworms in a flat-bottomed cage with absolutely no substrate whatsoever for one or two days a week.

Captive tarantulas may be expected to eat six or seven crickets, or a dozen mealworms, a week. Your tarantulas should have a few crickets or mealworms in its cage at all times except during pre-moult, moult, and postmoult. If you use mealworms, you should put your tarantula in the mealworm dish at least once a week to make sure that it can find them.

If you can't get food for your tarantula for several weeks you need not panic. They are capable of fasting for long periods of time without apparent harm (Baerg, 1958) as long as they have ready access to drinking water. This should not be used as an excuse for allowing one to starve through neglect, however. As food becomes more plentiful you should feed your tarantula more heavily to allow it to regain its vigor.

Be forewarned about the practice of trying to raise most or all of your tarantula's food in your home. It is not recommended unless you have a truly large collection of tarantulas, or you plan on being snowbound most of the winter. Crickets and mealworms *will* get loose occasionally, and a great deal of time and effort is involved in their care. One hobbyist who tried it soon found himself so busy maintaining his cricket ranch that he was unable to care for his tarantula. He was moderately successful in the fishing bait business, however! You can get detailed instructions for culturing both mealworms and crickets from your local county agriculture extension agent.

Arboreal tarantulas from the tropics may pose a special feeding problem. Since they seldom go to the floor of the cage, and crickets seldom climb to a spider's lair, your arboreal tarantula may not get all the food it requires.

The hobbyist has several courses of action to remedy this: He may drop live crickets into the spider's lair or he can catch wild insects which normally live in the upper levels of grass or brush (but remember to avoid areas sprayed with pesticides). In a desperate situation, very small lizards (American chameleons or wall lizards, for instance) can be put in the cage with the tarantula.

Cleaning. When to clean the cage is a matter of judgment on your part. In nature no one actually sweeps out the lairs. We don't really know how they are cleaned. In captivity tarantulas are copious web spinners, laying down sheets of silk while feeding (Illus. 27), moulting, just moving around, and during various phases of breeding. They frequently ball up all the webbing in their cages and deposit it in a corner as though they intended their keepers to remove it every Monday morning with the rest of

Illus. 27. Tarantulas are copious web spinners. They commonly spin a "tablecloth" in their cages while waiting for food, add to it while eating, and then dismantle it and roll it into a corner when finished.

the garbage! We presume that they do this in the wild also, depositing their garbage outside the burrow's entrance or burying it somewhere in the back, but no one has reported seeing this.

Because you have the responsibility for your tarantula's well-being you should remove this detritus as it collects. A total shakedown and cleanup of the cage probably shouldn't be instituted until matters reach serious proportions. The wild tarantula presumably occupies the same burrow year after year, perhaps its entire lifetime, with few disturbances. We do not know if frequent, complete upheavals would have adverse effects on them. Still, that should not be used as an excuse for slovenly housekeeping. Probably one of the safest guides is your nose. When the cage develops an odor assume that it is time for a cleaning. First, move the tarantula into another container; then discard the soiled substrate (bedding). Wash the cage with warm water and a few drops of mild dish soap; rinse it well with clear water. Then set it back up with new substrate.

PESTICIDES

Tarantulas are presumably just as sensitive to pesticides as any other animal. Therefore, the following rules and warnings are suggested in an effort to help you save your pet's life.

1. Wash very thoroughly, or take a shower, after using any pesticides, especially dog and cat flea powders.
2. Do not powder the dog and cat in the same building as the tarantula.
3. Keep your tarantula *at least* two rooms and one closed door removed from any of the common, plastic insecticide strips.
4. Remove your tarantula prior to spraying or fumigating for household pests and keep it away from the building for at least 48 hours.
5. Identify all government agencies which are likely to spray your neighborhood for mosquitos, flies, or other insect pests. Find out their spraying schedule and evacuate your tarantula at least one day in advance and keep it away until at

least two days thereafter. Alternatively, seal it, and its cage, in plastic bags as described below.

6. Don't smoke around your tarantula. Tobacco smoke contains nicotine, still one of the most potent insecticides known.

7. Don't feed your tarantula any animals which may have been exposed to pesticides.

There have been a very few instances where tarantulas have been exposed to presumably lethal doses of insecticides and survived. Either these animals did not get a fatal dose, or they had an inherent resistance to the pesticides used. If they did receive a sublethal dose we are unsure what the long-term effects will be. In any case, *don't take chances with your pets*. It is far better to be safe than sorry.

In a crisis you can seal your pet, cage and all, in a double thickness of plastic trash bags to protect it from poisoning. Tarantulas can survive a day or two sealed in like this because of their low oxygen demands. Do not blow into the bags to inflate them. Your breath contains a powerful poison, carbon dioxide, and the goal is *not* to kill your pet!

HANDLING

Yes, you can and should handle your tarantula! (See Color Illus. T and U.) One of the most often-stated purposes for keeping a tarantula is to show it to guests and friends. If you are accustomed to handling your pet, and it is accustomed to being handled, you will be able to carry off a much smoother performance in front of other people. This is not necessarily an exercise in vanity. The better you are at convincing the general public that you know what you are doing, and that the spider is nowhere near as dangerous as it appears, the better will be the chances of acceptance and appreciation of tarantulas and other "crawlies" by that same public in the future. Stripped of its euphemisms, it's propaganda pure and simple. Tarantulas need all the public relations help they can get!

In addition, frequent handling will keep your pet quite docile for those times when it *must* be handled, such as during cage cleaning and removal from pesticide sprays. You'll survive those crises better, too.

There are a few instances when you should not handle your tarantula except under the direst emergency, if at all. Among them are:

1. If it is sold as an unidentified species or as a questionably dangerous species. *It is not recommended that the rank amateur attempt to keep this type of animal.* If you have any doubts, seek professional help, and in the meantime use a scoop (an empty tin can or plastic drinking cup) to move the animal. Generally, any tarantula sold in a pet shop to the general public can be considered safe to handle. There are probably fewer than a dozen species in the entire world that may be dangerous; the author has seen reports of only two or three.

2. If the animal is overly aggressive. It may stridulate, rear back and lunge at you with fangs bared (Illus. 28), and turn to face you if you circle to get the advantage from behind. Use a scoop to return it to its cage to "cool off." If it exhibits this behavior repeatedly you should probably write it off as an intractable cage pet. For its safety, as well as yours, you should disturb it as little as possible and seek a different species as a pet. Of the thousands of tarantulas that the author has handled over the years this has only happened with two species: a large African baboon tarantula and some Haitian tarantulas (see Color Illus. S).

3. If the tarantula is showing signs of an imminent moult. At this point it should not be disturbed, or it should be moved *most gently* with a scoop. You can determine if it is about to moult by examining the bald patch on the top rear of the opisthosoma. If it is light tan or light brown the animal is not in premoult and is safe to handle. A dark brown or black area where the urticating bristles are missing indicates that it is about to moult. Do not handle your pet for at least a week or until after it has moulted and again accepted food, whichever is longer.

Illus. 28. This Haitian tarantula is attacking a wooden dowel. If you do encounter one of the very few aggressive tarantulas, it's best just to leave it alone.

The popular notion is that you should use your thumb and index finger across the middle of the prosoma, between the second and third pairs of legs, to pick up a tarantula (Lund, 1977; Perroro and Perroro, 1979; Browning, 1981). This method is very insecure and we strongly recommend against this practice.

There is not enough room between the legs for our fingers to fit comfortably, therefore we cannot obtain a secure grip on the animal without the danger of harming it. If a claw has hooked the substrate, the tarantula may be pulled from your grasp as you lift it. Or, if the animal is unaccustomed to being handled, it may struggle from your grasp. If you tighten your grip in an effort to prevent it from falling you may crush it because a tarantula's prosoma isn't constructed to resist lateral compression. If it does struggle free, it may fall to its death. Regardless of what happens, this is no way to impress your spectators.

A far safer method is to cup your hand slightly and come down gently over the tarantula's top as though you were picking up an egg. Your thumb should be placed beside the animal's pedipalps and chelicerae. Your index and middle fingers should come down over the tops and fronts of the chelicerae. The animal's body should be cupped into the palm of your hand with the remainder of your fingers underneath, preventing its escape. If it struggles, you are in a position to prevent its fall. If it tries to bite, your fingers are safely out of the way, but in a position to subue the action of the chelicerae and fangs. And, it doesn't appear as though you're terrified of the animal. (See Illus. 29–31.)

Don't drop your tarantula! A fall of more than a few inches will almost always kill a tarantula. If your friends are squeamish about tarantulas do not allow them to handle your pet except on a tabletop. At first this might also be a good rule for you. Hopefully, this will prevent a tragedy.

Don't blow or breathe heavily on your tarantula. Its instincts immediately identify you as a predator and it will either jump or broadcast those urticating bristles, or both.

About those bristles: You should probably handle a tarantula before you purchase one. If you are the one-in-a-hundred who breaks out in hives from contact with them you might want to think twice about keeping a tarantula as a pet. These hives seldom last more than a day, but they can be spectacular. The other ninety-nine will only suffer a mild itching for a few hours. Washing your hands immediately after handling your pet will help prevent any itching. Just be careful not to touch your face around your eyes before you wash your hands.

Don't scare people with your tarantula! Shoving a huge hairy spider under someone's nose may seem like a cute prank and may be well nigh irresistible, but it jeopardizes your pet, opens you up to serious liability suits, and is bad public relations for both tarantulas and you. Any way you look at it, it's just plain cruel.

A surprising number of people are arachnophobes—that is, they have an overpowering, deep-seated, irrational fear of spiders. Attempts by the amateur to treat or cure such a condition may result in serious emotional problems for the victim as well as a

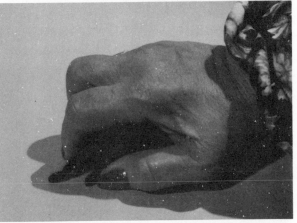

Illus. 29–31. Picking up a tarantula. This sequence of photos illustrates the recommended procedure. One way of describing the action is to compare it to picking up a fragile egg. Note that the animal ends up securely cupped into the palm of the hand, and the fingers are not endangered by the fangs.

fractured friendship. Leave the problem to the professionals. When you encounter such a person merely sympathize, and keep your tarantula away.

BITING

Once they are accustomed to being handled, pet tarantulas almost never bite, and with very few exceptions neither do the wild ones. Even if one does bite it seldom injects venom, and the wounds are little more than needle pricks. They may usually be treated with a mild antiseptic and a small bandage.

Even if venom is injected the effects are minimal. The comparison has been made to a bee sting but there is little resemblance. A bee sting immediately swells, itches, turns red, and burns. A tarantula envenomation develops more slowly, turns red, may not swell at all, and usually only aches or tingles. It should be noted here that conflicting reports do occur in the literature (Baerg, 1922 and 1925; Bucherl, 1968–1971; Maratic, 1967). The symptoms given here are from actual bites received by the author and his wife from several "Haitian" tarantulas (four with no reaction and one mild reaction), a wild "woolly Honduras" tarantula (no reaction), and an unidentified species from the Rio Grande Valley of Texas (mild reaction) (see Color Illus O). Worldwide there may be fewer than a dozen really dangerous tarantulas and none of them are native to the United States. It is important to stress that these several bites occurred over a span of some fifteen years, while handling and selling thousands of tarantulas.

If you are bitten by an unidentified species, or are violently allergic to insect bites and stings, or are acutely hyperallergenic, you should contact your physician or local poison control center. If any suspicious symptoms arise, call an ambulance or have a friend drive you to an emergency clinic. *Do not drive yourself!*

Tarantula venom is a very low-grade, dilute neurotoxin and normally doesn't require any treatment. Recent investigators have determined that the venom of a common North American species closely resembles scorpion venom (both scorpions and spiders are members of the class Arachnida), and probably would be just as virulent if it were produced in similar concentrations (Stahnke and Johnson, 1967).

It is remotely possible for acute hyperallergenics to suffer varying degrees of anaphylaxis, a far more serious condition. Currently no tarantula antivenin is being produced in the United States, as there is simply no reason for it. An Australian laboratory may be producing a type which works against the venom of several related Australian spiders, but the delay in acquiring it makes it worthless in an emergency here, assuming that it was necessary in the first place. It is questionable if the black widow antivenin currently available in the United States would work against a tarantula's envenomation.

Under no circumstances should you allow the injection of any antivenins until a sensitivity test has been run on you. If you are allergic to the horse serum from which they are made, the cure is surely more serious than the bite!

All this sounds far and away more terrible than it really is. None of the tarantulas commonly sold in pet shops are considered dangerous. As was pointed out earlier, they rarely attempt to bite, seldom inject any venom, and the symptoms of an envenomation develop very slowly and seldom reach noteworthy proportions. To date, the author is unaware of any fatal tarantula bites in the United States (Parrish, 1959). It is questionable if most doctors would even know what to do in the case of an envenomation, so rare are they.

KINDS OF TARANTULAS

Although no attempt will be made to scientifically identify any species here, the following list itemizes some of the commonly sold tarantulas in the United States. These refer specifically to juveniles and mature females. Mature males are short-lived and normally far too nervous to be recommended as pets.

Southwestern Tarantula. Several species from the southwestern United States. Usually dark brown to black with a tan carapace. Inexpensive. Very docile. Excellent pet. (See Color Illus. R.)

Haitian Tarantula. Drab brown with a pinkish iridescence on the carapace. They are seldom docile, and long-term captives may remain intractable. Prone to bite when wild. Inexpensive. (See Color Illus. S.)

Woolly Honduras Tarantula. Dark brown to black with numerous curved, light tan bristles on the legs and opisthosoma. Not very docile when newly caught, but readily tamed. Moderately expensive. (See Color Illus. I.)

Mexican Red Leg. Probably better termed "orange knee" as there is a species with far redder legs. Black and tan with bright orange markings on the leg joints. They are docile, even when wild. Excellent pet. Expensive but well worth the price. This one has particularly irritating bristles. From Colima, Mexico. (See Color Illus. H.)

Pink-Toed or Orange-Tipped Tarantula. Possibly two species. Dull black to jet black with a bluish, gunmetal iridescence on the carapace. Pink or orange tips on the tarsi and pretarsi. Nervous but easily tamed. Not prone to biting. Displays the interesting habit of building a tubular web in the vertical corner of its cage. Prefers to rest, prosoma downwards, in this nest. Probably a rain forest species and arboreal in nature. Possibly requires a higher humidity than the desert species. Moderately priced. From northern South America. (See Color Illus. A.)

Guatemalan Black Velvet Tarantula. Jet black with a sprinkling of long, bright red hairs on the opisthosoma. Very docile, but expensive. Not commonly available because of the current political conditions in Central America. (See Color Illus. J.)

MEDICAL PROBLEMS

We don't know much about the medical problems of tarantulas. They are so different from more familiar animals that it is difficult to draw analogies or work from parallel cases. Thus we can only use some guesswork and a little background knowledge to try to effect a cure. We know that they die, but few people (and mostly hobbyists, at that) have tried to find out why. Few have actually tried to cure an ailment.

Below, we discuss what little is known of their maladies.

Moulting Problems. Before proceeding with this discussion it is probably best to stress again that a tarantula that has turned upside down (i.e., is lying on its back) is definitely *not* dying or dead! This is a normal prerequisite to moulting. Dead tarantulas remain upright with their legs folded underneath them somewhat in the manner of a clenched hand (see Color Illus. M).

Moulting is the most critical act that your tarantula performs. Once your tarantula begins to moult it must complete the process or die. If you notice that your pet is having a great deal of difficulty emerging from the old exoskeleton you can help it if you are very careful. First, be absolutely certain that it is having difficulties, and not just resting. If it cannot free itself after ten or twelve hours you may safely assume the worst and proceed to help.

Try to acquire a small bottle of pure glycerine from a pharmacy or grocer. Caution: This is neither glycerine and rose water, nor nitroglycerine (for *angina pectoris* in people). If it is unavailable proceed without it. Start by mixing a solution of one teaspoonful of glycerine to two cups of room-temperature tap water. Then you must thoroughly wet the tarantula with this solution and keep it wet for several hours. *Don't move the animal unless it is absolutely necessary!* Gently drip the glycerine solution on the spider with an eyedropper, but try not to get any of this solution onto the book lungs as it might drown your pet. This will soften the exoskeleton so that you and your pet can deal with it without injury. After six or eight hours, if your pet still hasn't moulted, you may try to remove the carapace and/or sternum, but only if you are very careful not to puncture the tarantula, and only after the plates are thoroughly soaked with the glycerine solution. You probably should not attempt to remove the exoskeleton from the legs unless absolutely necessary because of the danger of dismembering the animal. But you may try to remove the exoskeleton from the opisthosoma. Be particularly careful about injuring the tarantula's book lungs. During the entire operation you should be using a pair of good quality, blunt-tipped forceps or tweezers.

After a bad moulting a tarantula may not eat for several weeks. Do not despair. The tarantula may be having trouble with the lining of its mouth, pharynx, and pumping stomach, which are normally shed with the old exoskeleton. If that is the case, there isn't much that you can do except allow the animal to work out its own problem. Tarantulas can fast an amazingly long time if they are given water and were in good physical condition in the first place.

One thing should be mentioned at this point. In nature tarantulas spend most of their time in their burrows, especially just prior to moulting. These burrows not only afford mechanical protection from enemies and the elements, but also maintain a higher humidity around the animal than is normally encountered in captivity. This higher humidity undoubtedly has a beneficial effect on the tarantula's moulting by helping the old exoskeleton to remain more pliable before it is cast off. Thus we suggest the practice of lightly misting your pet daily with room-temperature tap water from an atomizer or plant sprayer during the few days of premoult. Do not use glycerine at this point, however. Be careful not to drench the animal or its cage. Caution: Be certain that the atomizer or sprayer is thoroughly washed before use. Be especially careful about pesticide contamination.

Injuries. If your tarantula's armor is ruptured it may "spring a leak." This is most common during moulting, or if the spider is handled too roughly or dropped. The hemolymph which seeps out will dry to become a clear amber scab. If the injury is on the legs merely put the animal back into its cage and do not handle it for four or five weeks to allow time for it to heal. You must still offer it food and water. The scab will be removed by the tarantula at the appropriate time or will be cast off with the next moult. *Don't remove it yourself.*

A rupture on the prosoma or opisthosoma is a crisis of the greatest proportions. Our philosophy is that it is better to try to save the animal and fail, than not to try at all; therefore we offer these suggestions as an experiment only. The hobbyist must realize that the damage was already done, and he must accept the consequences as his own.

Of paramount importance is stopping the flow of hemolymph. You might try to improvise a bandage of unscented toilet tissue or very soft paper (kitchen) towel. Normal adhesive bandages and tapes won't work because of all the bristles.

The absorbent paper bandage is intended to hold the rupture together and to allow a firm matrix for scab formation. This same technique, using rice paper, is reportedly used by the Chinese peasantry on their own injuries. If the opisthosoma is widely ruptured you might consider taking the animal to a veterinarian, if you can find one who is broad-minded enough! The veterinarian might be able to suture the rupture together because the exoskeleton on the opisthosoma is very leathery. He must be very careful not to disturb or puncture the internal organs, just the exoskeleton. He must also use a very fine suturing material which will automatically dissolve away because of the impossibility of removing it once the exoskeleton begins to knit. Any remaining sutures will seriously interfere with subsequent moults.

Nothing is known of the dosages or effects of lidocaine (lignocaine), ether, halothane, or any other anaesthetic on tarantulas except that they will kill if overdosed. Therefore they should not be used. If anaesthesia is necessary to control the animal merely cool it for a few minutes in a refrigerator. Be careful, freezing is fatal!

Another suggestion is to dust corn starch, flour, or pure unscented talcum powder on the wound. The theory is that it will absorb the escaping hemolymph and become a foundation for a developing scab. We have no way of knowing what effect perfumes or other adulterations may have on tarantulas, thus it is best to avoid them if at all possible.

An antibiotic ointment, such as Mycitracin® Antibiotic Ointment (bacitracin, polymyxin, and neomycin) manufactured by the Upjohn Company, or a similar product, should be applied to forestall infection. These are available at any pharmacy without a prescription. Never use any of the strong disinfectants such as iodine, Merthiolate®, Mercurochrome®, alcohol, or peroxide. They will surely poison your pet.

After such major surgery *do not handle your pet until after the next moult, and only after it again starts to eat!*

Vermin. Rarely, a hobbyist reports an infestation of tiny white or tan mites in a tarantula's cage (Browning, 1981). While these mites are not parasitic they are an unsightly nuisance and may irritate your pet. They arise when the cage is being kept too moist and can be eliminated with a thorough cage cleaning.

Remove the tarantula to another container and throw away all the old cage contents. Wash the cage with a solution of one-fourth cup of chlorine bleach per gallon of water. Rinse the cage well until there is no smell of chlorine. Allow the cage to air dry at least for a day. Set the cage up for your tarantula with new substrate, but this time keep it desert dry. Be sure to supply a dish of clean water. Rain forest species cannot be kept in such dry conditions longer than four or five days, however, without danger of death from dessication. For them, a new cage with all new decorations and plants is recommended.

Never attempt to eradicate the mites with any pesticide!

A similar problem concerns tiny, bright red or orange mites which frequently infest scorpions from the American Southwest. Occasionally, a tarantula will be found with a few of these attached. Most of them will detach and wander off if the tarantula is placed in a very humid container. Any mites remaining on the animal may be picked off *carefully* with a pair of high-quality forceps, or brushed off with a dry cotton swab. The author has seen no reports of these forming an infestation in captivity. If one did occur it should probably be treated the same as the mites described earlier.

ESCAPES

What do you do if your pet escapes? The very first thing is to usher both the cat and the dog out-of-doors. Both are likely to try to eat the tarantula if they find it, and both the eater and the eaten will suffer.

Next, you must examine tarantula psychology carefully. They are confirmed acrophobes. Not only do they seldom climb, but if they perceive themselves to be "up" they almost invariably try to get "down." The key word here is "perceive." Tarantulas have such limited powers of perception that they instinctively assume that any horizontal surface under them is "down," even if it is the top shelf of a bookcase in the attic. Tarantulas are normally also recluses. Even males will hide during the light of day, and females and juveniles will hide in a dark place almost indefinitely.

Tarantulas have very limited long-range senses. They are not attracted by what they may see, smell, or taste. Therefore, you cannot bait them. Neither will they return to their cage for they simply have no way of finding it except by blind chance.

To find a lost tarantula you will need a good flashlight (torch) and a mechanic's mirror. This is a small mirror swivelled on a long handle, and it is used for seeing into difficult places. Other tools may be necessary depending on circumstances.

The chances are excellent that the tarantula is within twelve inches of the floor, hiding in some dark recess, in the same room where it escaped. Choose some convenient landmark, a doorway for instance, and systematically search the room, always going to the right (or left). Be extremely cautious about shifting things until you have looked around them to make certain that you won't crush your pet. Don't slide books into a shelf without searching behind them first. Don't open reclining chairs and hide-a-bed sofas until you have inspected their mechanisms.

The key to finding your pet is the thoroughness of your search. You must be very careful to look into every nook and cranny that a tarantula might squeeze into, and they are amazingly adept at concealing themselves. Check inside the cheesecloth bottoms of sofas and easy chairs. Don't ignore the spaces inside the arms of these, also. Look into any hot- or cold-air registers that you might be able to squeeze your finger into. Carefully look into all boots and shoes. Inspect the full length of floor-length drapes, as the tarantula might have assumed it was in an extra long burrow when it found a fold. Don't miss the clever little false bottoms that many items of furniture conceal. Look into stereo cabinets and speaker housings, and into the insides of radios and televisions if they are near the floor. You must also check behind all drawers in bureaus, dressers, and cabinets. If you don't find it the first time take a break. Then search the same room again, even more thoroughly.

If the second search didn't reveal your pet, move to the next room and do it all over again, twice. Tarantulas will go down stairs, but seldom up. If you can't find it on the floor where you lost it, search on the next lower floor. Search once a day until you find it.

After retrieving your pet *don't put it back into its old cage!* It has already demonstrated its ability to escape from it. Either reconstruct the old cage to prevent further escapes or get a new, escape-proof one. Having to crawl all over the house on your belly to find your pet spider is hilarious, but forgivable, the first time. Having to do it twice is inexcusable stupidity.

6
Catching Your Own

Occasionally, through design or accident, the hobbyist will find himself in a position where he has the opportunity to collect his own tarantulas. The following comments are offered to help the amateur collector.

WHERE TO COLLECT

You cannot simply walk out into any random field or pasture and pluck a tarantula from under a rock. In North America they are found generally west of the Mississippi River and south of the 38th parallel, but there are exceptions. Within that range their distribution is spotty and somewhat unpredictable.

On a more local scale, they are found on rather high, dry land. You will never find a colony in a swamp or marsh, or in an area that floods frequently. You may find their burrows out in the open, as well as beneath large rocks, hummocks of grass, or under shrubbery. They prefer soil which is firm and capable of maintaining a solid burrow. Thus, you will probably not find them in sand, gravel, or very loose soil. Neither will you ever find them on land that has been tilled any time in recent history—it simply takes too long for them to set up housekeeping.

The entrances will be neat, nearly perfectly round holes. During inclement weather they may be covered with a thin veil of silk but shouldn't be littered with dirt or dead leaves. During warm weather, if you see such a burrow with an indistinct, radiating web at its entrance you may have struck "pay dirt," but these are also produced by many other kinds of spiders.

PARAPHERNALIA

The recommended equipment list is not too long: a pair of leather gloves, a small garden trowel, a stout tablespoon, a collection of plastic containers with lids, and as many gallons of water as you can carry. A potato rake is optional but very handy; it is used for turning over logs and rocks from a safe distance. The water is used to flush the tarantulas out of their burrows. The plastic containers are for carrying your catch. The trowel and spoon are for digging. The gloves are to protect your hands from sharp rocks and scorpions. The gloves which work best have a thick lamb's wool piling in them—a protection that is well worth the bother, even in the heat of summer.

TECHNIQUES

There are basically three techniques used to catch tarantulas. First on the list is to simply dig the animals out of their burrows when they are found. This has four serious drawbacks: it's hard work, it's terribly time consuming in the hot sun, you stand a very good chance of killing the tarantula if you aren't *extremely* careful, and your excavations can lead to serious erosion.

The method of digging that works best for the author involves some strategy. First, find a grass straw some eight to twelve inches long, and then gently probe into the burrow to determine if it is more or less straight and vertical or which way it bends or slopes.

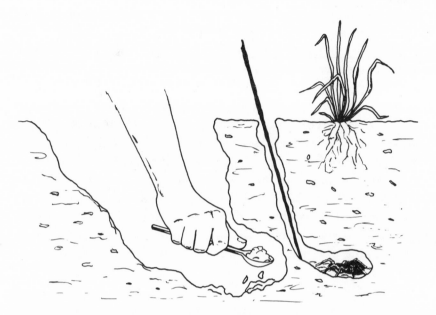

Illus. 32. Digging out a tarantula (*see the text for details*). After digging up a tarantula burrow, you must firmly tamp the soil back into the hole to prevent disastrous erosion.

Next, dig a small pit some ten to twelve inches away from the burrow's entrance and on the side *away* from the slope or bend. When your pit is some twelve or more inches deep carefully excavate sideways, from the bottom third, to intersect the tarantula's burrow. Extreme caution must be used at this time to insure that the burrow isn't crushed, and the tarantula isn't killed. Careful removal of all loose soil with a tablespoon is of paramount importance to avoid burying the animal alive. When the lower portion of the tarantula's burrow is thus exposed, the spider can be carefully teased out with the grass straw or spoon handle (Illus. 32).

After removing the tarantula you must carefully refill and tamp the disturbed soil back into the pit. Such holes, left exposed, will act as foci of erosion in the chaparral, causing irreversible damage. When you dig, you automatically assume the obligation to protect the habitat of the animals you prize so highly. If you cannot accept that responsibility, *don't dig!*

The second technique is to pour large amounts of water into their burrows to flush them out. This has the advantage of not tearing up the landscape, but it is awfully tiring to lug all those gallons of water all over the desert.

To implement this technique, again find a grass straw eight to twelve inches long and probe the burrow, but leave the straw in place. Then carefully fill the burrow with water (Illus. 33). As the water level slowly recedes watch for the tips of the tarantula's forelegs protruding from the surface several inches down the burrow. At this point, careful prodding with the grass straw (already in place) will encourage the tarantula to exit its burrow. While prodding, it is usually helpful to stand so as to shade the burrow's mouth with your body as the spiders intensely dislike the bright light. Some practice is necessary to become proficient, but well worth the effort.

If no tarantula appears or if it dives back down the burrow in-

Illus. 33. The author flushing a tarantula from its burrow. Note the protective gloves, long sleeves, and long pants.

stead of exiting, flood the burrow again. If you aren't successful after the third flooding, find another hole. If the burrow never fills with water it probably connects to a large crack in the subsoil, a common condition, and further flooding or digging is futile.

The third method is to drive very slowly down side roads after dusk ("road cruisin' ") with your car's headlights turned on. You may find many tarantulas using this method, but they will probably be males. You will also find an amazing assortment of other types of animals too, many of which are dangerously venomous (e.g., rattlesnakes, scorpions).

While you are in the field you must be very careful to keep your newly caught tarantulas out of direct sunlight. Not only are they very uncomfortable in bright light, but they also will be cooked by the heat. When you get them back to your car you must also be extremely careful. As the desert temperature soars above 100° F. (38° C.), your car's internal temperature can skyrocket into the cake-baking range! The same is true even in a city parking lot. It's the same sun either place.

WHEN TO COLLECT

Usually tarantulas can be hunted and collected at any time of the year. However, two periods in the year (for North America) pose special collecting problems.

In the colder months, the tarantulas are semidormant and unable to escape their burrows. During these times, attempts to flood them from their burrows are futile and may only drown them. Digging is then the method of choice, providing the disturbed soil is replaced and firmly tamped after removing the animal.

In the months of July and August (again, for North America) tarantulas are normally moulting. During these times they likewise may not be able to leave their burrows. They may also be extremely fragile until they complete their moulting cycle. Do not be too persistent about trying to flood them out, and be especially careful while digging for them and handling them.

TRANSPORTATION

The containers which work best for carrying your tarantulas are sixteen-ounce plastic freezer boxes. The next best are common plastic cottage cheese cartons. You should put your newly caught pets into these cartons and supply them with a few air holes for ventilation. When you get back to civilization you should put a small wad of wet absorbent cotton (cotton wool) into each box.

If you are going to ship them long distances you should put these individual cartons together in the center of a larger cardboard box and cushion them with about one and one-half inches of packing on all sides, including the top and bottom. Crushed newspaper or "plastic peanuts" are the best packing material. (Plastic peanuts are small bits of plastic foam used specifically for packing delicate cargo.)

At the time of this writing the author knows of many people who ship their tarantulas through the mail. Before you do this, you should check postal regulations with your local postmaster. If you cannot mail your tarantulas you will have to use one of the independent freight agencies. Look in the yellow pages of your local telephone directory for their names and locations. You should probably not try to ship them during freezing weather.

CAUTIONS

There are two facets of tarantula-collecting that you must be aware of. First, many national and state governments have restrictions or prohibitions against the collection, exportation, or importation of wildlife. Before you begin to collect tarantulas you should consult with local authorities. If you choose to break the law the consequences can be severe. For instance, many countries are now treating such cases as poaching, with the same penalties as drug smuggling! Beware!

Second, never trespass on private property without the owner's permission. If you cannot find the owner, collect elsewhere. Cattlemen are perpetually suspicious of rustlers, and landowners are very defensive of their property. Trespassers are sometimes shot on sight, even in the twentieth century, even in the United States!

SAFETY

You must be ever careful of your own safety. To list all the pitfalls of "field-tripping" would take volumes. Instead we suggest three basic rules and then offer an example.

1. Do not take undue risks. Avoid hazardous situations; and if you find youself in an awkward predicament, take the coward's way out! Be careful not to overexert yourself or overextend yourself.
2. Go prepared for the terrain and climate. Always wear long-sleeved shirts as protection against the sun, weather, insects, and spiny or irritating plants. In venomous snake country wear reasonably snake-bite-resistant boots. A hat is suggested in the heat of day to prevent sunstroke. A container of water is recommended if you are planning to go far from civilization. A first aid kit and the minimal training necessary to use it are also highly recommended.
3. Always take a buddy. Always tell someone where you are going and when you plan to be back.

An Example. On a collecting trip to the chaparral of south Texas the novice can expect some nasty surprises. In such an area virtually every plant is bedecked with spines or thorns. Temperatures commonly go over 100 ° F. (38 ° C.) in the summer and well below freezing in the winter. A cloudburst many miles distant can turn your arroyo-campground into a swirling maelstrom.

The creatures of the prairie and chaparral are many and varied, and most of them have some effective method for defending themselves. If you don't recognize the animal you've found, give it a wide berth. Diamondback rattlesnakes are common, as are black widow spiders (see Color Illus. Q), scorpions (Illus. 34), velvet ants, fire ants, blister beetles, and a host of other unwholesome creatures.

Illus. 34. Tarantula relatives: a common scorpion of Texas. Order Scorpionida. Venomous. This is one creature you want to avoid when collecting tarantulas.

Never stick your fingers into places that you haven't carefully inspected first; tarantulas have dangerous bedfellows. The same clump of grass which shelters the tarantula's burrow may also conceal a black widow spider. The same rock which acts as the tarantula's roof may also protect a scorpion. And the shrubbery shading the tarantula's lair may also camouflage a cactus.

Never stand *in front of* the rocks and logs that you are lifting. Stand behind them and lift them towards you so that they may protect you from the lunge of an irate rattlesnake. It's a mean world out there!

ECOLOGICAL ETIQUETTE

A very important point which you must acknowledge is that, as a naturalist, you are merely *harvesting* an important, renewable, natural resource. This implies that you have the responsibility neither to plunder nor rape the landscape for the animals you seek. These habitats are far too fragile to survive such abuse. Instead, wherever possible you should purposely try to produce and improve more habitat. Ripping up a 150-year-old shrub to get a tarantula is sheer folly. Pouring noxious chemicals down burrows to roust out the inhabitants is idiocy. And littering the landscape with a host of craters from digging is unforgivable.

Instead, always replace turned stones and logs, and reposition any others to allow more habitat sites. If you must dig, do so conservatively, and replace and firmly tamp all turned soil when you are finished.

If you locate a colony of tarantulas do not exterminate it. Merely *harvest* a few and allow the others to live in peace. At the same time try to improve the habitat to allow more living space.

Be very cautious about allowing others to know the location of such a colony. All your finest efforts can be ruined by one thoughtless, ruthless fool.

Only the most boorish dolts witlessly scatter their waste over the landscape. Unfortunately, the world seems replete with them. Do not become a part of that group. Instead, carry along a plastic trash bag. In it you should not only put your own trash, but you should try to clean up the mess left by our slovenly brethren.

MUSEUM SPECIMENS

It would be a good idea to send a specimen or two to a major museum from each collecting site, but you must include collection data with them. These include your name and address, the date of collection, the place of collection, and any notes which you wish to include about the animal's habitat. The date should be of the form: 14 April 1983, not 4/14/83. The place of collection should include country, state or province, county or parish, and nearest city or town if available. Additionally, an approximate distance and well-defined direction from that town or city is very desirable (e.g., fifteen miles south of Del Rio on U.S. Highway 277, Val Verde County, Texas).

Professional scientists usually attach a collection number to each specimen and keep a logbook in their pockets in which they make notes on the specimen's ecology, natural history, and habitat. That log number may then be attached to corresponding photos. Later, back in the laboratory, the scientist transfers the number and information into a formal register which becomes part of his collection system. When specimens are donated to museums, or sent to other scientists for study or identification, they are accompanied by the collection number and any information recorded in the register, including duplicates of the photos. The serious collector is urged to adopt a similar system. It is only through such a formal record system, executed with nitpicking accuracy, that we can gain really precise information about these animals in nature and in captivity.

If you wish to ship live tarantulas follow the directions given earlier. If you wish to ship dead, preserved ones, you have the problems of killing them humanely and preserving them. Probably the most humane method of killing a tarantula is simply to put it in the refrigerator for several hours to cool down. The next step is to transfer it to the freezing compartment. Presumably, it goes numb and feels no pain as it gets cold since tarantulas are cold-blooded and experience the same phenomenon in nature during cold weather. When you put it in the freezer it is unconscious and doesn't experience any discomfort during death.

The best method for preserving one is to "pickle" it in alcohol or formaldehyde. Both of these are obtainable from local high school and college biology labs, many pharmacies, and chemical supply houses. You should use 90% denatured ethyl alcohol or grain neutral spirits, not isopropyl rubbing alcohol. Biology teachers can supply you with sources and addresses if you must buy materials through the mail.

Do not ship preserved specimens in liquid. After they have soaked for several weeks in the preservative you should carefully drain off all the excess liquid and ship them in a moist condition. Wrapping them in soft paper (kitchen) towels, moistened with preservative, inside tightly sealed, sturdy glass bottles will protect them from damage and keep them from drying out. You should ship only one specimen to each bottle, but several bottles can be wrapped in one package. Be sure to protect them with lots of padding both from each other and from the walls of the box. Each specimen *must* be accompanied by its own accurate label. Each label *must* be with its specimen *inside* the bottle. Each label *must* be printed in lead pencil—even waterproof inks will smear or fade in these preservatives.

Such museum specimens serve as the starting point for nearly all tarantula research. They are the most important part in the process of learning about these intriguing spiders.

7

Breeding
Tarantulas

CAVEATS

Successful attempts to breed tarantulas are almost unknown.
The "great-grandfather" of tarantula keepers, William Baerg, apparently was unsuccessful at getting them to mate, lay eggs, and
have the eggs hatch in captivity. All the eggs that he procured
were from newly caught females that had been impregnated in
the wild (Baerg, 1938). And, sad but true, after more than forty
years we still do not know much more than Baerg—hardly more
than the basic requirements.

Obviously both sexes are needed. A new male must be acquired
every year since they seldom live much longer than nine months
after they have matured. Several males are recommended in case
one is sterile or impotent.

Since there is no easy way to distinguish between juvenile
males, juvenile females, and mature females, the prospective
breeder may have to maintain a large number of tarantulas in the
hope of getting the required number of breeders.

The author was once a party to an attempt to breed tarantulas where everything occurred by the book, except that some four or five weeks later "she" moulted into a truly gorgeous male!

We don't know why tarantulas do not breed readily in captivity. Baerg thought they required beetles in their diet (Baerg, 1958), and the author noted that various beetles, mainly tenebrionids and carabids, were exceedingly common under stones in the deserts of south Texas where tarantulas are also quite common. But there is some question as to whether they require a variation in diet or if beetles have some magic property for tarantulas. If they do, what could it be?

Other conditions may also effect breeding, such as light intensity, temperature, moisture, substrate, handling, and time cycles (diurnal, lunar, seasonal, and annual). If we knew each species' exact origin, especially the exotic species', we might be able to guess at reasonable parameters for these variables. We might also be able to guess at other conditions that could have an effect.

Obviously, the larger the number of specimens the more you can vary the conditions, but large collections of tarantulas can be expensive to amass and time consuming to maintain. The hobbyist must bow to his own limitations.

One possible solution to the problem might be a cooperative effort by a group of hobbyists. But do not allow the lack of resources to stop you from trying on your own if the opportunity presents itself.

TECHNIQUE

The male tarantula should have built his first sperm web shortly after his maturing moult. They are normally very secretive about it, so the only evidence that you might have is an otherwise clean web rolled up in the corner. You may try to use him for breeding anytime after you suspect that he has built one, or anytime after about two weeks following his maturation, whichever comes first. The female is ready to breed most of the time, as they apparently do not suffer a "heat" period. But be forewarned that it is futile to have a female bred if she is approaching the moult-

ing season (July and August in North America) because the linings of her spermathecae and any semen which they hold are shed
with the rest of her exoskeleton. North American tarantulas
usually mate in the fall (September and October), and there is
good evidence that some of the Central American species do also.
Little is known about the breeding seasons of the many exotics,
however.

Those males which shed the previous fall are probably too old
and weak to mate by the following spring, but those which may
mature in the spring are vigorous and willing through the entire
summer.

The breeding cage must be large enough to allow for free movement because the male has to be able to outmaneuver the female.
A ten-gallon aquarium is sufficient. You must make certain that
the female has been well fed for several weeks prior to mating lest
she prefer dinner to sex. Place the male near the female but not
touching her. If he does not take the initiative after several minutes gently nudge him closer until he touches her. If all goes well
he will perform his nuptial duties without hesitation, even in
public. It is possible that he will be more willing to mate if the female's cage is used as the breeding cage because it will "smell"
more feminine. We don't have enough experience in the matter to
tell for certain, however.

If possible, photograph and time the entire spectacle. Keep a
log describing exactly how you set them up, what you did, how
they reacted, what they did, and all the time spans involved. The
more information you record, the better. If you are successful you
will want to write about it or at least have these notes to refer to
when you try again. We don't know enough about the details of
the mating habits of the various species except to suspect that
they do differ. Nor do we know if different species are capable of
hybridizing. How can we? We haven't yet found the secret of
breeding two tarantulas of the same species!

Be prepared to separate the two spiders, especially towards the
end of copulation when the male is trying to make good his escape. Use a piece of thin cardboard, not your hand. Not only
might you be too clumsy but you might also be bitten by the fe-

male. Be gentle! The female is seldom really intent on eating the male and you might injure either or both if you are too forceful.

Use each male with as many females as possible, including those belonging to your friends. Little or nothing is known of the fertility rates in tarantulas and this practice will weight the odds a little more in the favor of a successful breeding. Swap wives, so to speak. Use the males to their fullest, every three or four days, whether you see a sperm web or not—a short life, but a merry one!

MATERNITY CARE

The author has first-hand knowledge of only one successful breeding of a tarantula in captivity. A friend, John Blue, purchased the female Mexican red leg (orange knee) tarantula on October 23, 1976. Mr. Blue arranged a mating with a male on December 3, 1976, and again on January 9, 1977. The female was kept in a five-gallon aquarium on a one-to-two-inch-thick layer of potting soil. On March 25, 1977, she produced an ootheca.

Thereafter, the female and her ootheca were misted with tap water from a house plant sprayer three or four times a week to maintain humidity. The temperature was maintained at 75 ° F. to 80 ° F. (24 ° C. to 27 ° C.)

Mr. Blue allowed her to retain the ootheca until June 14, 1977. On that date, out of curiosity, he removed the ootheca and slit it open to expose the eggs. They were translucent white and were showing some dark pigmentation.

Since the female was acquired in the fall of the year after the onset of their presumed mating season there is the possibility that she was bred in the wild by another male tarantula. This is a strong argument in favor of using several males because if one was sterile the other obviously wasn't. It is also possible that the resulting spiderlings are a "mixed litter," with some of them having one father and the others having a second. If the female had been bred by a third male, some of the spiderlings could possibly also be from him.

The fact that Mr. Blue used potting soil in the "maternity ward" undoubtedly contributed to the survival of the eggs because numerous attempts made by other individuals failed when the eggs dessicated. Frequent use of the plant sprayer was of at least equal importance.

Baerg (1958) states that somewhat higher temperatures are required to ensure the hatching of the eggs. Thus the somewhat elevated temperature at which the eggs were kept was also lucky.

PEDIATRICS

The eggs hatched five days later, on June 19, 1977. Thus their incubation period was about 86 days. About 1,180 spiderlings emerged. Within a very few weeks they began to cannibalize each other. To prevent this they were transferred to individual one-ounce plastic condiment cups (with lids to prevent escape) of the sort used in fast-food restaurants for tartar sauce. A little potting soil was added to each cup to hold moisture. The spiderlings were fed baby crickets. Instructions for breeding crickets are available from county agriculture extension agencies and entomology departments at major universities. Wingless fruit flies might also work. They and their directions for culture are obtainable from biological supply houses, high school biology labs, and university zoology and genetics labs. Laboratory assistants, teachers, and professors can supply you with the addresses for mail order supply houses.

The fact that Mr. Blue opened the ootheca prematurely may also have been fortunate. This allowed the spiderlings to escape their cannibalistic siblings sooner than otherwise, thus allowing many more to survive. Removing the ootheca from the female is probably also a good idea as female tarantulas frequently destroy their egg cases in captivity (Baerg, 1958). The ootheca should then be kept in an "incubator" that will allow both high humidity and good ventilation. Perhaps a one-quart glass canning jar, with one or two inches of slightly damp potting soil and a screen or mesh lid, would be ideal.

Do not be too quick to pass judgment on an unhatched ootheca. We know absolutely nothing about the effects of differences in temperature or moisture on development rate. Neither do we know the incubation time of most species. If we take Mr. Blue's lead and maintain a relatively high humidity and temperature, and carefully cut a small escape hatch in the ootheca, there is no reason to give up hope for the eggs until at least the end of six months. Even then the eggs should be carefully examined for signs of development before being discarded.

All tarantula fanciers are deeply indebted to Mr. Blue for both his pioneering efforts at attempting such a breeding, for his foresight in keeping detailed notes of his actions, and for his kind permission to report the results here.

In Mr. Blue's hatching the spiderlings grew at least as fast as in the wild. At age four years they spanned one and one-fourth inches and had developed adult color patterns (Illus. 35).

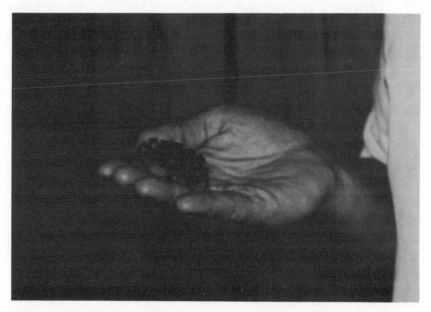

Illus. 35. Paul Christ holding one of John Blue's baby tarantulas. The spider is only four years old here.

Baby tarantulas should probably be watered and fed at least once a week. As they grow they should be moved to larger quarters, perhaps pint or quart canning jars at first, then gallon mayonnaise jars from restaurants. You should try to handle them as soon as practical. The sooner they become accustomed to the human hand the better they will adjust to captivity. Your major goal at this time should be to produce well-adjusted breeders as the nucleus of a captive colony.

The successful hobbyist is advised to keep only fifty to seventy-five of the spiderlings. The rest can be distributed to other hobbyists. Be forewarned: No information is available regarding growth rates and sex. You should *not* keep only the largest.

You should keep accurate, detailed records of their development. The minimum should include the identity of several specimens; when they moult; what, how much, and how often they eat; and their cage or room temperatures. If possible, photograph them against a ruler and weigh them with a sensitive laboratory balance after each moult. Such balances may be found in nearly all high school and college chemistry and biology labs, and the teachers or professors can show you how to use them. A complete set of labelled and dated cast skins would also be helpful.

A record should also be kept of all who receive your extra spiderlings. As your tarantulas mature, contact your associates and arrange for crossbreeding with their specimens, thus completing the cycle and continuing the project.

SUMMARY

The care of tarantulas is very simple because they are such hardy, undemanding creatures. Indeed, most of the instructions are "DON'TS"—prohibitions to protect your pet. They are also relatively safe to handle and make most interesting pets.

Unfortunately, we do not know enough about their demands to be able to predictably breed them in captivity, and any zoo keeper will vouch that breeding is the sign of a truly contented and well-cared-for animal.

Herein lies the greatest and most important challenge for the hobbyist. A truly successful, long-term breeding program will have at least four important results. First, it will ease the collecting pressures on the natural populations.

Second, it will offer the opportunity of conserving rare species or those which are very difficult to obtain.

Third, it will increase the availability of these most interesting pets to you, the hobbyist.

Fourth, the complete breeding habits of one or more species will at last be known, and another piece of the puzzle will be placed.

8
You Can Help

AN ADMISSION OF ABJECT IGNORANCE

A persistent theme throughout this book has been that we know far too little about tarantulas. Only a few people have ever really studied them, and very little of the information gathered so far has been corroborated by other researchers. What we do know only leads us to ask more questions.

While hundreds of theraphosids have been scientifically described, only one or two species have been intensely studied. All that we know of the others is their physical descriptions and collection data. Their phylogenetic relationships and taxonomy are so far out of date and so confused that no one is even certain how many species there actually are. To date, no one has made a concerted effort to publish a comprehensive key to the genera and species, and it is doubtful that anyone could until this chaos is corrected.

IS THE CAVALRY COMING?

What can be done to remedy this situation? As a hobbyist you can do a great deal to solve our problem of ignorance. Here are some suggestions.

1. Support national hobbyist organizations. Become a member. Offer your financial help or backing. Offer your physical help (work) in operating the organization.
2. Start your own local organization, but keep it very simple and informal (complex organization and petty politics *always* ruin a good club). Chief among its goals should be the support of a responsible national organization.
3. Experiment *gently* with your pets.
4. Try to breed your pets.
5. Keep accurate records of all of your observations.
6. Write articles about your experiments and observations.
7. Try to educate the general public with school programs and other demonstrations.
8. Raise funds for scholarships for budding arachnologists.
9. Become a professional arachnologist yourself.
10. Raise funds to sponsor research by professionals.
11. Lobby government agencies for those projects which will help to preserve areas that contain tarantula colonies.
12. If you are fluent in a second language, make arrangements to translate foreign language scientific papers into English so that your cohorts may also benefit from them.

MAYBE NOT!

At this point a word must be said about two national hobbyist organizations which have dealt with arachnids in general, spiders in particular, or tarantulas specifically.

The first is The National Arachnid Society and its associated Spider Museum. This organization was started by one very enthusiastic individual, existed for some time, and achieved a large measure of success. Unfortunately, at the time this book goes to press this organization is not active. This happened because not enough people were willing to assume the work and responsibility for the organization, and those who did simply were unable to bear the full burden.

The second organization is The American Tarantula Society

(publishing the *Tarantula Times* magazine), and it tells much the same story. The work (and much of the expense) involved in running the organization is being borne by only a very few. Because of the monumental demands placed on the people involved, the organization has had a very tenuous existence. For reference, the address is:

The American Tarantula Society/*Tarantula Times*
24 Country Ridge Drive
Huntington, CT 06484

What can be done to help? Go back and read the list of suggestions given above. We cannot afford to lose hobbyist organizations such as these because of lack of interest or neglect. If we wish to reap the rewards of such an effort, *we* must expend the effort! There is no such thing as a free lunch, and there is too much to lose.

9
Publish! Publish! Publish!

For most people, the thought of writing an article for publication instills a terror second only to going to the dentist. Yet, this is the only means that the rest of the world has of knowing what you have seen or done. If you have something to say, you say it, don't you? Well, why not write it?

If you are writing as a professional you are outside the scope of this discussion and should consult biology departments at colleges and universities for guidance. As a hobbyist, however, you may submit your material to any of the publications issued by your club or any other. You will doubtless find out about them by talking with other tarantula fanciers (whom you may meet in pet shops, for instance).

If you have good 35 mm transparencies, many popular nature and sporting magazines would be interested. You may find their names and addresses in their publications at the larger newsstands or in special listings at your local library. Some publishers of books for the pet industry often buy such photos. Their names and addresses are available in their publications in pet shops or lists of publishers at the library. Ask your prospective publisher for his requirements. He will be glad to offer suggestions.

But how do you write an article? As a start, get a piece of paper, take a pencil firmly in hand, and write down the first word. Follow it with the second. Good! You've now mastered the most difficult part. Don't give up now. *Keep going!* Don't worry about punctuation, spelling, or grammar. The most important step is to get it all down in black and white before you get cold feet.

You will probably have to rewrite it two or three times before you get it right, but you needn't be too fussy at first. Eventually you should end up with a neatly handwritten or, better still, typed copy. While you should make some effort to use correct English, don't let that stop you. The publisher will have an editor or proofreader go over your article to correct the errors.

While your masterpiece can be in letter style, most publishers prefer essay style. Number your pages and make sure that your name and city appears in the top left corner of each page. Your full name and address should go on the first page. Don't forget to include a cover letter telling the publisher that you are sending him this material in the hope that he will find it interesting enough to print.

Write as simply and as compactly as possible. Very long sentences will try your publisher's patience. Don't despair if you have questions or trouble writing because free help is very plentiful. Your local library will have many books and pamphlets giving detailed instuctions on everything from correct spelling to the fine points of writing prose. Just ask the librarian where to find them. Many English and literature teachers in public schools will gladly spend several hours with you if you ask them for help. Have faith, your first endeavor is always the hardest. Once you've published you'll catch "the fever."

Never think that what you have to say is too dumb or of little interest. Let the publisher worry over that. If you fail to report a fact because you prejudged it as insignificant it will never stand a chance of getting printed. There are few details about a tarantula's life that are too trivial to be told.

Tell it all. Tell it like it is!

Bibliography

This is not an exhaustive list of all books and articles on tarantulas. The interested reader will find that many of these sources also contain bibliographies which will in turn refer him to still more references.

Many of the entries in this bibliography are not mentioned in the text. The reader is advised to look this bibliography over carefully and refer to any articles, books, or periodicals which appear to hold the information sought. If your local library does not have the item that you need, you may be able to order it through an interlibrary loan system.

Nearly all of the periodicals mentioned here will continue to publish for many years to come. If you are interested in keeping abreast of the field or are seeking more up-to-date information you are well advised to find current issues and the last several years' indexes.

Anderson, J. F. 1966. "Excretia of spiders." *Comp. Biochem. Physiol.* 17:973–982.

Baerg, W. J. 1922. "Regarding the habits of tarantulas and the effects of their poison." *Sci. Monthly.* 14:481–488.

——— 1925. "The effects of the venom of some supposedly poisonous arthropods of the Canal Zone." *Annals Ent. Soc. Am.* 18:471–478.

————— 1926. "Regeneration in the tarantula *Eurypelma californica* Auser." *Annals Ent. Soc. Am.* 19:512–513.

————— 1928. "The life cycle and mating habits of the male tarantula." *Quart. Review Biol.* 3(1):109–116.

————— 1938. "Tarantula studies." *Jour. N. Y. Ent. Soc.* 46:31–43.

————— 1958. *The Tarantula.* Univ. Kansas Press. Lawrence. (Father of tarantula books. Out of print and hard to find.)

————— 1963. "Tarantula life history records." *Jour. N. Y. Ent. Soc.* 71:223–238.

————— 1970. "A note on the longevity and moult cycle of two tropical theraphosids." *Bull. Brit. Arachnol. Soc.* 1:107–108.

Blackwelder, R. E. 1963. *Classification of the Animal Kingdom.* Southern Illinois Univ. Press. Carbondale.

Bonnet, P. 1957. *Bibliographia Araneorum.* 7 vols., Toulouse (Independent). (In French. Includes exhaustive listing of all scientific papers dealing with spiders through 1938. Includes one classification scheme.)

Browning. J. G. 1981. *Tarantulas.* TFH. Neptune, N.J.

Bucherl, W., et al. 1968–1971. *Venomous Animals and Their Venoms.* 3 vols. Academic Press. N.Y. Vol III, "Spiders," 197–301.

Buchsbaum, R. 1948. *Animals Without Backbones.* Univ. Chic. Press. Chicago.

Buckley, S. B. 1862. "The tarantula (*Mygale hentzi* Girard) and its destroyer (*Pompilus formosus* Say)." *Proc. Ent. Soc. Phila.* 1:138–9.

Burdette, Walter (editor). 1974. *Invertebrate Endocrinology and Hormonal Heterophylly.* Springer-Verlag. N.Y.

Butler, W. H. and B. Y. Main. 1961. "Predation on vertebrates by Mygalomorph spiders." *West Australian Naturalist.* 7:52.

Caras, R. 1974. *Venomous Animals of the World.* Prentice-Hall. Englewood Cliffs, N.J. (Interesting pictures.)

Cazier, M. A. and M. A. Motenson. 1964. "Bionomical observations on the tarantula hawk wasps and their prey (Hymenoptera: Pompilidae: *Pepsis*)." *Ann. Ent. Soc. Am.* 57:533–541.

Cloudsley-Thompson, J. L. 1967. "The water-relations of scorpions and tarantulas from the Sonoran Desert." *Entomologist's Monthly Magazine.* 103:216–220.

———— 1968. *Spiders, Scorpions, Centipedes, and Mites.* Pergamon Press. London.

Comstock, H. and W. Gertsch. 1948. *The Spider Book.* Cornell Univ. Ithaca, N.Y.

Cook, J. A. L. 1972. "Stinging hairs: a tarantula's defense." *Fauna, The Zoological Magazine.* 4:48.

Cook, J. A. L., V. D. R. Roth and F. H. Miller, 1972. "The urticating hairs of Theraphosid Spiders." *Am. Mus. Novitates* #2498. (Very good article. Types of bristles vs. tarantula species. Some insights into habits and behavior.)

Den Otter, C. J. 1974. "Setiform sensilla and prey detection in the bird spider *Sericopelma rubronitons* Ausserer (Araneae, Theraphosidae)." *Neth. Jour. Zool.* 24(3):219–235.

Ellis, C. H. 1944. "The mechanism of extension in the legs of spiders." *Biol. Bull.* 86:41.

Firstman, B. 1954. "Central nervous system, musculature and segmentation of the cephalothorax of a tarantula *Eurypelma.*" *Microentomology.* 19:14–40.

Gertsch, W. J. 1979. *American Spiders.* Van Nostrand. N.Y.

Gertsch, W. J. and H. K. Wallace. 1936. "Notes on new and rare American Mygalomorph spiders." *Am. Mus. Novitates.* 884:1–12.

Ghiretti-Magaldi, A. and G. Tamino. 1977. "Evolutionary Studies on Hemocyanin." *Structure and Function of Haemocyanin.* Edited by J. W. Bannister. Springer-Verlag. Berlin.

Kaston, B. J. and E. Kaston. 1953. *How to Know the Spiders.* Brown. Dubuque, Iowa.

Linzen, B., D. Angersbach, R. Loewe, J. Markl, and R. Schmid. 1977. "Spider Hemocyanins: Recent Advances in the Study of Their Structure and Function." *Structure and Function of Haemocyanin.* Edited by J. W. Bannister. Springer-Verlag. Berlin.

Loewe, R., R. Schmid, and B. Linzen. 1977. "Subunit Association and Oxygen Binding Properties in Spider Hemocyanins." *Structure and Function of Haemocyanin.* Edited by J. W. Bannister. Springer-Verlag. Berlin.

Lund, D. 1977. *All About Tarantulas.* TFH. Neptune, N.J. (Interesting caging arrangement suggested. Excellent photography.)

Manton, S. M. 1958. "Hydrostatic pressure and leg extension in Arthropods." *Ann. Mag. Natur. Hist.* (13)1:161–182.

Maratic, Z. 1967. "Venom of an East African Orthognath spider." *Animal Toxins.* Eds. F. E. Russel and P. R. Saunders. Pergamon Press. N.Y.

Meglitch, P. A. 1972. *Invertebrate Zoology, Second Edition.* Oxford Univ. Press. N.Y.

Minch, E. W. 1978. "Daily activity patterns in the tarantula. *Aphonopelma chalcodes* Chamberlain." *Bull. Brit. Arach. Soc.* 4(5):231–237.

———— 1979. "Reproductive behavior of the tarantula *Aphonopelma chalcodes* Chamberlain (Araneae: Theraphosidae)." *Bull. Brit. Arach. Soc.* 4(9):416–420.

Parrish, H. M. 1959. "Deaths from bites and stings of venomous animals and insects in the United States." *A. M. A. Archives on Internal Medicine.* Vol 104, August.

Parry, D. A. and R. H. J. Brown. 1959. "The hydraulic mechanism of the spider leg." *Jour. Exp. Biol.* 36:423–433.

Perrero, L. and L. Perrero. 1979. *Tarantulas In Nature & As Pets.* Windward Press. Miami. (Good starting book.)

Petrunkevitch, A. 1911. "Courtship in tarantulas." *Ent. News.* 22:127.

———— 1926. "Tarantula versus tarantula-hawk: a study in instinct." *J. Exp. Zool.* 45:367–397.

———— 1952. "The spider and the wasp." *Sci. Am.* 187:20–23.

Platnick, N. 1971. "The evolution of courtship behavior in spiders." *Bull. Brit. Arach. Soc.* 2:40–47.

Rao, K. P. and T. Gopalakrishnareddy. 1962. "Nitrogen excretion in Arachnids." *Comp. Biochem. Physiol.* 7:175–178.

Roewer, C. F. 1942–1954. *Katalog der Araneae.* Kommissions-Verlag von "Natura." Bremen. (In German. Lists most synonyms for spiders' scientific names. Presents one taxonomic scheme.)

Savory, T. H. 1928. *The Biology of Spiders.* Sidgewick and Jackson. London. (Out of date, but still informative.)

———— 1964. *Arachnida.* Academic Press. N.Y. (Good overview of arachnids, but very little on tarantulas.)

———— 1977. *Arachnida.* Academic Press. N.Y. (Revision of the 1964 edition. Both are listed here due to important changes.)

Schmidt-Nielsen, K. 1975. *Animal Physiology.* Cambridge Univ. Press. N.Y.

Slama, K. and C. M. Williams. 1965. "The juvenile hormone v. sensitivity of the bug *Pyrrhocoris apterus* to a hormonally active factor in American paper-pulp." *Biol. Bull.* 130:235–246.

Smith, C. P. 1908. "A preliminary study of the Araneae Theraphosidae of California." *Ent. Soc. Am.* 1(4):207–249.

Snodgrass, R. E. 1952. *A Textbook of Arthropod Anatomy.* Comstock. Ithaca, N.Y.

Stahnke, H. L. and B. D. Johnson. 1967. "*Aphonopelma* tarantula venom." *Animal Toxins.* Eds. F. E. Russel and P. R. Saunders. Pergamon Press. N.Y.

William, F. X. 1956. "Life history studies of *Pepsis* and *Hemipepsis* wasps in California (Hymenoptera: Pompilidae)." *Ann. Ent. Soc. Am.* 49:447–466.

Wood, F. D. 1926. "Autotomy in arachnida." *Jour. Morph. Phys.* 42(1):143–195.

Zoological Record. Zoological Soc. of London. (Exhaustive listing of all zoological scientific papers. Arranged by taxonomic group. Refer to sections on arachnids.)

Index

Note: Page references listed as letters refer to the section of color photographs that begins opposite page 32.